WEREWOLF
MAGICK

© Denny Sargent

About the Author

Denny Sargent (Aion 131, Hermeticusnath) is a writer, artist, and university instructor. He has a bachelor's degree in education and a master's degree in history and intercultural communications and has been involved in international education most of his life. He has written several university textbooks and sets of international curriculum.

In the magickal world, he has been an initiate of or an accepted member of a number of esoteric traditions and groups including, but not limited to Welsh Traditional Craft, Church of All Worlds Church of the Eternal Source, the Typhonian OTO, Nath Tantrika Lineage, the Grove of the Star & Snake, Voxas Rimotae, the Voodoo Spiritual Temple, the Shinto Kamisama and Priests, the Horus Maat Lodge, and Coven of the Mystical Merkaba. Denny has written for a number of magazines and anthologies in the United States and Japan, and has written books and articles on Paganism, Western occultism, spells, folklore, magick and tantra extensively. His published books include *Global Ritualism, Myth & Magick Around the World, The Tao of Birth Days, Your Guardian Angel and You, Clean Sweep, Banishing What You Don't Need, The Book of the Horned One, Naga Magick,* and *Dancing with Spirits: Festivals & Folklore of Japan.* He was a coauthor for *The Book of Dog Magic* and *The Magical Garden.* He has had three limited edition grimoires published as well: *Liber Sigil A IAF, Liber Phoenix,* and *Liber Eos.* He is Elder Guardian of the Horus Maat Lodge and has edited and written parts of two books for the LodgeHML: *The Compleat Liber Pennae Praenumbra, The Horus Maat Lodge Book,* and *The Grimoire of a PanAeonic Magickal Tribe.*

Denny lives in Seattle where he gardens, tutors adults with autism (including his son), travels internationally as much as possible, and has a wonderful dog named Faunus. More information can be found at www.dennysargent author.com and on Instagram at @dennysargentauthor.

WEREWOLF MAGICK

AUTHENTIC PRACTICAL LYCANTHROPY

DENNY SARGENT

Llewellyn Publications
Woodbury, Minnesota

FIRST EDITION
Fourth Printing, 2023

Cover design by Kevin R. Brown
Developmental editing by Brandy Williams
Interior art by Llewellyn Art Department

Llewellyn Publications is a registered trademark of Llewellyn Worldwide Ltd.

Library of Congress Cataloging-in-Publication Data
Names: Sargent, Denny, author.
Title: Werewolf magick : authentic practical lycanthropy / Denny Sargent.
Description: First edition. | Woodbury, Minnesota : Llewellyn Publications,
   [2020] | Includes bibliographical references. | Summary: "Lore tells us
   you can either be born a werewolf or become one through magic. However,
   this book explains that there is a third way to become a werewolf, one
   that combines magic, psychology, and working with your etheric or astral
   energetic body. Combining history and practical exercises, this book
   will help readers unleash their inner beast"— Provided by publisher.
Identifiers: LCCN 2020023286 (print) | LCCN 2020023287 (ebook) | ISBN
   9780738764450 (paperback) | ISBN 9780738764610 (ebook)
Subjects: LCSH: Shapeshifting. | Werewolves. | Magic. | Rites and
   ceremonies.
Classification: LCC BF1623.M47 S27 2020 (print) | LCC BF1623.M47 (ebook)
   | DDC 133.4/3--dc23
LC record available at https://lccn.loc.gov/2020023286
LC ebook record available at https://lccn.loc.gov/2020023287

Llewellyn Worldwide Ltd. does not participate in, endorse, or have any authority or responsibility concerning private business transactions between our authors and the public.

All mail addressed to the author is forwarded but the publisher cannot, unless specifically instructed by the author, give out an address or phone number.

Any internet references contained in this work are current at publication time, but the publisher cannot guarantee that a specific location will continue to be maintained. Please refer to the publisher's website for links to authors' websites and other sources.

Llewellyn Publications
A Division of Llewellyn Worldwide Ltd.
2143 Wooddale Drive
Woodbury, MN 55125-2989
www.llewellyn.com

Printed in the United States of America

Other Books by Denny Sargent

The Book of Dog Magic

Global Ritualism

Acknowledgments

This book would not exist and neither would I if it weren't for my pack of loving and wild friends. If we have howled together, this means you. Special thanks to those who helped me with editing, proofreading, and inspiration: the amazing author and editor Brandy Williams, the talented feral artist Vasco Brighi, and the creative and stalwart Peter Carr, and much honor and thanks to my loving feral friends from many circles including the Horus Maal Lodge, the Ordo Templi Orientis, Golden Dawn, and my beloved Coven of the Mystical Merkaba. Also, a shout out to the werewolf band Man with a Mission for a cool writing soundtrack—*domo*!

From my feral heart I dedicate this book to my wild nonverbal autistic son, Forrest, who taught me the meaning of perseverance and that truth and love need no words. Also, to my little wolf, Faunus the doggo, who reminds me daily that all us animals instinctively live, die, hunt, play, and are wholly one within nature.

Finally, this book is an offering of love to the great Wolf Spirit and all the beautiful endangered beasts: may their cries and howls fill our hearts and awaken us to halt the slaughter and save the Wildness, and so save ourselves. Join all us beasts in this great work as you will, with love. So may it be.

Contents

List of Exercises, Rituals, Spells, and Rites ... xiii

List of Photos and Figures ... xv

Disclaimer ... xvii

Preface ... xix

Introduction ... 1

Chapter 1: History, Lore and Werewolf Cults ... 9

Chapter 2: Principles of Werewolf Magick ... 27

Chapter 3: Werewolf Magick Tools ... 47

Chapter 4: Freeing Your Inner Wolf ... 79

Chapter 5: Shape-Shifting ... 101

Chapter 6: Fetch Work ... 127

Chapter 7: Werewolf Rituals ... 141

Chapter 8: Werewolf Magick with the Dead ... 157

Chapter 9: Werewolf Magick Spells ... 171

Conclusion: The Final Howl ... 197

*Appendix A: A Theoretical Reconstruction of a Medieval
   Full-Transfer Shape-Shifting Ritual ... 203*

Bibliography ... 207

Exercises, Rituals, Spells, and Rites

Chapter 3

The Growl / Sway Exercise ... 70

Blessing Ritual for Werewolf Magick Talismans and Tools ... 73

Chapter 4

Calling the Wolf Spirit Exercise ... 80

Werewolf Dream Spell to Meet Your Inner Wolf ... 83

The Deep Wolf Scrying Exercise ... 88

Finding Your Wolf-Self Spell ... 90

Awakening Your Inner Werewolf Spell ... 92

Werewolf Restrictions Release Rite ... 95

Chapter 5

Wolf-Power Exercise ... 101

The Praxis Shifting Rite ... 106

Wildness Shape-Shifting Ritual ... 109

Advanced Wildness Shape-Shifting Ritual ... 117

Chapter 6

Calling Forth and Shape-Shifting the Fetch Exercise ... 129

Building Up the Fetch Exercise ... 131

Exercise to Create a Fetch Shrine ... 133

Sleep Fetch Work Exercise ... 136

Chapter 7

Hekate Lunar Wolf Spirit Ritual ... 141

Solar Werewolf Empowerment Ritual ... 146

The Divine Wolf Star Ritual ... 148

Lupus Dei Ritual to Defeat Evil Sorcerers or Entities ... 152

Chapter 8

Werewolf Spell to Learn of the Past or Future from the Dead ... 158

Rite to Travel a "Deadway" and Meet with a Shade of the Dead ... 160

Ritual for Honoring and Guiding the Dead with Anpu ... 165

Chapter 9

Invocation of Faunus Lycan ... 171

Werewolf Power Candle Spell ... 173

Werewolf Magick Lunar Holy Water Spell ... 176

Attracting a Werewolf's Love Spell ... 180

An Abramelin Werewolf Spell ... 182

Eyes of the Wolf Spell ... 185

Spell to Make Someone Shut Up ... 187

Werewolf Berserker Spell ... 189

Popping Claws Protection Spell ... 191

Lunar Eclipse Purification Spell ... 193

Photos and Figures

Photo 1: Werewolf Altar ... 52

Figure 1: The Triskele ... 59

Figure 2: The Wolf Paw ... 59

Figure 3: Werewolf Fangs ... 60

Figure 4: The Eye of the Wolf ... 60

Figure 5: The Claw Slash ... 61

Figure 6: The Pentagram (in paw) ... 61

Figure 7: The Lit Stang ... 62

Figure 8: The Triple Moon ... 63

Figure 9: The Wolf Triquetra ... 63

Figure 10: The Eye of the Wolf ... 85

Figure 11: The Algiz Rune ... 94

Figure 12: The Sirius Sigil ... 149

Figure 13: Raido Rune ... 158

Figure 14: Ankh ... 166

Figure 15: Abramelin Square ... 185

Figure 16: Isa Rune ... 187

Figure 17: Berserker Rune ... 189

Figure 18: Wolf Triquetra ... 201

Disclaimer

This book is intended for adult use only due to the contents of some of the exercises and rituals. Handling or consuming raw or undercooked food may increase your risk of foodborne illness, especially if you have certain medical conditions. The publisher and author assume no liability for any injuries caused to the reader that may result from the reader's use of content contained in this publication and recommend common sense when contemplating the practices described in the work.

PREFACE

————— +|+ —————

I have always been into werewolves, and if you've picked up this book, I'm guessing you are too. As a kid, I loved the old classic werewolf movies and, being a wild child, delighted in roaming and howling in the woods with my pack of feral friends. I grew up, as we all must, and I put such things aside. I had an adult life. There were joys and tragedies, and I enjoyed a kind of normal and mundane life for a couple of decades.

Then, suddenly, I was hit by a completely unexpected total personal disaster.

Without warning, I lost my home, my art studio, my temple, my job, my savings, and even my dog. I was utterly despondent and alone and depressed and traumatized beyond belief. I felt I was finished with this life. I ranted and prowled and felt like a monster, numb, useless until a friend said something to me that stuck in my head: "Embrace your monster!"

Something inside me awoke with a jolt, a part of me I'd suppressed and ignored most of my life. Something wild and vital broke through the despair. Everything suddenly shifted. What the hell was happening? My inner beast, my monster, was suddenly howling at me to heed the instincts I had switched off all my life. I couldn't sleep or be still. I stopped thinking and just ran with it.

I grabbed camping gear and some simple food I had like raw veggies and nuts. *Fresh raw meat,* my inner beast said. I grabbed that too. Without much of a plan I drove up into the mountains and ended up in a national forest at an isolated campground. I turned the car engine off and rested my head on the steering wheel. What the hell was I doing?

I began screaming, howling out my anger, fear, frustration, and dark red pain. I couldn't stop, I was letting go, I was flying apart. Finally the eruption calmed and I entered a weird, post-freak-out listlessness. I was silent, in body, in mind, in self.

My animal instincts took over. I grabbed my stuff and stumbled to a campsite I was near. *Eat*, my inner beast said. I stumbled out and sat on a log. I ate some nuts, drank some water, and breathed in the green surrounding me. I finally noticed it was warm and sunny.

You don't need these, my inner animal said, prompting me to throw off my clothes. Guided by instinct, I found a large mossy stone where I laid bloody raw meat and a cup of pure water. I called wordlessly to the Lord of the Forest, to Mother Earth, and—I wasn't sure why at the time—to the Wolf Spirit to accept my offerings.

As it got darker I built a fire. I had nothing, no clothes, no words, no thoughts. Even the gods were silent. All I had was despair. The stars came out. I felt the moon rising.

The beast within me raged for release. I howled with my whole being, metaphorically ripping myself open to let the monster out. I howled to the great Wolf Spirit and the primal wildness all around me. I howled and howled and howled into the dark forest until I was hoarse, exhausted, and utterly empty. It was silent. Then, from the surrounding mountains, a single howl answered me.

A terrifying flood of wild energy and animal fierceness filled me. My desperate call had been accepted by the great Wolf Spirit. All the hair on my body stood on end. I began growling, over and over, deeper and deeper, embracing the Wolf Spirit and letting it fill me. I let my beast within tear its way out. With a shocked shudder of horror and relief I knew what I really was. I began to sob in utter relief.

When the full moon rose through the trees I howled a different song. This time it was not pain, sorrow, or desperation, but a full-body acceptance of being an animal, a human-wolf, wholly and completely. I howled my release and my joy at embracing the fierce intensity and deep feelings of the Wolf Spirit. I embraced my inner monster.

I slid into pure animal consciousness, remembering little except fuzzy flashes of memory. I rocked and danced and growled about the fire. When I slid into my sleeping bag I was shaking with electric energy. It was as if I physically changed into a wild hairy beast. A werewolf, of course! The wilderness and I became one. It was orgasmic. Everything faded to darkness except for the animal consciousness that consumed me.

In the morning I awoke with a start and leapt from my bag vibrating with energy. Everything had changed. I saw the forest truly for the first time, every detail of light and shadow, every tree and stone. I was filled with strange information about living as an animal-human in the world, a werewolf. I was finished suppressing the Animalself within me, my beast. Now the wolf-power shared my soul, my skin, my life.

When I visited the mossy rock where I had put the food and water, they were both gone. The Spirit of the Wolf had accepted the offerings—had accepted me.

I cleaned the campsite and drove home to explore my new life. Then I started writing.

I understood that my new life had begun when I started connecting to my Animalself. So many of the issues and wrong turns in my life had come from suppressing my monster, from trying to civilize my inner beast to being proper instead of authentic. I vowed never to suppress it again.

I spent every day walking in parks and in forests, growling and listening to my Animalself. Then, my Animalself showed up in my dreams and meditations as a three-eyed werewolf. He said, "Write. It will come. I will help. I'll show you. Call it werewolf magick." I laughed out loud! How absurd! Yet, here we are.

I grew my beard in, spent more time in nature, spent more time growling and howling, and tried to understand this wild and magick uncharted path that my inner wolf was leading me down. I understood that the roots of self-destruction lay in forgetting we were animals, imprisoning our Animalself, through which we'd lost our connection with nature. I began to howl, dance naked in the woods, and try out every werewolf ritual pouring out of me. In this way werewolf magick grew from my crazy beast-self trying to piece together my wild werewolfery in words. I felt like a werewolf trying to type with big clumsy paws and I'm sure I scared a few people who wondered what the hell was howling out in the forest at 2:00 a.m.

It's been three years. I am now a hairier and happier beast and I look and feel years younger. I tend to growl a lot, but all in all, I am a better human for being more animal-like.

I believe I have uncovered and woven together the essential truths behind werewolves, shape-shifting, and its practical application for modern ritualists who are willing to dance with their inner beast. I was helped by dear friends, authors of obscure texts and a lot of researchers who had bits of the truth for me to gnaw on.

My inner wolf just rolls all his eyes as I type this. Yeah, I know, *blah blah blah*, animals don't need books. Yeah, but we poor suppressed humans do. So here it is, a paperbound piece of my wild heart for you. May it help you embrace your beast with freedom and joy.

In Wildness,
Denny Sargent
Full Moon, 12.12.19

INTRODUCTION

This is a book of fur and fangs and howls. It is a book of wildness and illogic, for it is a book of wild gods and spirits, of full moon revels, beasts and werewolves. In fact, this book exists to help free you from the constraints of a civilization that has forgotten the primacy of nature and denied the truth that we *are* animals. The goal of this book is not only to help you remember your innate wildness and animal powers, but to show you how you can unleash them. In the process, I truly believe, you'll become happier, wilder, freer, more authentic, and more open emotionally, physically, and psychically, for all of these are rooted in your Animalself, your inner wolf, the beast you have been forced to suppress and deny most of your life. I believe that when we connect to our Animalself and to nature, it restores our compassion for the earth and drives us to care for it.

Werewolf magick is a form of animalistic primal magick rooted in shape-shifting traditions, mostly from areas where wolves were apex predators and important spiritual beings. Werewolf magick focuses on magickal, psycho-logical, and spiritual shape-shifting—shifting from a human mindset to a low-er-cortex, centered feral consciousness—by unleashing the Animalself within and so manifesting as a "man-wolf" or what we now call "werewolf" forms. You can see this kind of animal magick in ancient pictographs, myths, and magickal lore, but the techniques for such shamanic lycanthropy—the taking on of animalistic consciousness manifesting as wolfish characteristics—are often obscured or hidden. I have done my best to rediscover these practices and try them out. They work, but in ways that may be unexpected, as you will see.

Ancient tales tell of a time long ago when all humans could converse with and learn from the animal spirits, our primal ancestors. Some tribal cultures I've visited, such as the Maya in Guatemala and the Mien in the Thai mountains, still do these things. However, the Western culture I find myself in seems to have lost the ability because social norms and religions have arisen that convinced us that we are not animals and are separate from nature. Today, as we approach ecological disaster, we see where this fallacy has led us.

My hope is that the information about historical werewolf magick, shape-shifting, and ritual practices will help us revive and embrace our Animalself to be happy and to reconnect as aware animals with our environment, our Mother Earth, whom I will refer to as Gaia from now on

The goal of this book is to make you a happier, more aware animal-person, what the ancient Norse called a "wer-wulf" or human wolf. This is a real, achievable goal. Shape-shifters have existed for thousands of years and there are still shape-shifters around today. I've met them.

This is not a book on shamanism; however it is informed by knowledge I received from shamans in the Siberian Ulch culture. I believe ancient Norse shamans and other ancient cultures used similar techniques for consciousness shifting with an animistic focus, just as the Ulchi do today. Since these techniques are mostly lost to us now, I am seeking to take the information I received and apply it within a Western historical framework. I understand that I am not a shaman and I hold the shamans I have met in my travels in high esteem and learned much from speaking and studying briefly with them. I believe the shamanic techniques I learned from real, practicing shamans can be used to unleash the Animalself as long as the rituals are done with focus and clarity. I believe you will be amazed at the results and will have a lot of fun unleashing your Animalself, as well as discovering the joys of pragmatic shape-shifting. One thing I can guarantee, you have never read a book quite like this.

How to Use This Book

I strongly suggest that you read the chapters of this book in order. Think of it as a long tutorial or a class you're taking on becoming a werewolf. Each chapter, in sequence, prepares you for the next chapter. If you skip around the book you will be missing both the experiences and the information needed for successful shape-shifting later on.

In general, the first part of the book gives you lots of important background information on werewolf magick, including history, principles, key ideas, tools, and techniques. This is all stuff you'll need to know in order to make later rituals work. Then the book shifts to more hands-on practices, exercises, rituals, and spells where you can apply what you have learned in an increasingly intense and complex manner. Again, just hopping into a ritual in the middle of the book will likely not work out well and will be confusing unless you have worked through all the steps that led up to and inform that ritual.

The last part of the book, where we get into spells and rituals, is quite eclectic and this is where you can hop around amongst the varied spells and rituals as you like if you have mastered what came in the chapters before.

Why Wolves and Werewolves?

Shape-shifting magick has often focused on top or "apex" predators like wolves. It makes sense if you think about it. One of the top predators in the ancient world were wolves. This later became even more true in northern climates and Pagan cultures. It made sense to become the most powerful animal available. It still does. Wolf shape-shifting offers ferocity, stamina, pack-like loyalty, intelligence, and power. Wolf gods and spirits were honored for centuries in such Pagan cultures and even today their ancient beliefs and rituals permeate our stories, festivals, and now movies and video games. As a kid I was fascinated by werewolves and their lore as I devoured Greek, Norse, and Celtic mythology. As I grew up and leapt into Witchcraft and magick I never lost my love of wolfish beings. So when my life blew up, in retrospect, it was not surprising that my Animalself emerged howling as a werewolf. Werewolf magick may not be for everyone, but since you're reading this, I'm guessing it works for you.

Are Werewolves Real?

Is magickal human-wolf shape-shifting real? In my experience it is and reviving this magickal system in a modern spiritual framework is the basis of this book.

I think you'll be surprised to see how many werewolf-oriented cults, covens, and sorcerers there have been throughout history in many different cultures.

Are in-the-flesh werewolves real? In the sense of "real wolf men who erupt with fangs and claws and a lot of hair every full moon," I am doubtful. That whole look seems antisocial, messy, and painful to me, though even today a quick search of social media sites will lead you to hundreds of "real" werewolf sightings, some with video and photographic "evidence." Such things are entertaining and there are true believers.

Throughout history, there have been many kinds of scientific and medical explanations concerning lycanthropy. Oftentimes, the belief someone has of being a werewolf is considered a symptom of a mental health illness such as schizophrenia, psychosis, hysterical neurosis, or manic depression. Some of the storied characteristics of a werewolf—like sensitivity to sunlight, excessive amounts of hair, and incisor teeth deformities—could be symptoms of a rare blood disease called porphyria.

Other characteristics thought to be related to werewolves could also be a symptom of congenital hypertrichosis universalis, a rare syndrome where one is covered with excessive hair often covering their face and body.[1] There is also folklore about children who were raised by wolves and became wolflike in nature and powers, like Mowgli in *The Jungle Book*.

Overall, Western materialistic and scientific views give no credence to werewolves and shape-shifting. Such creatures have been relegated to horror movies, Halloween costumes, and comics. On the other hand, wolf powers and wolves as "totems" have all become popular in new age, occult, goth, and furry circles. It is easy to find werewolf books, websites, and YouTube videos of all kinds, from serious spiritual views to amusing silly instructions on "ways of becoming a sexy werewolf." Eyeliner and leather are crucial, it seems.

Becoming a Real Werewolf

There is something deeper about werewolves than memes and tropes and that is why we are fascinated with them. You will see that for much of human history werewolves have been seen as important spiritual entities, aspects of pri-

---

1. The Complementary Medical Association, "Werewolves: A Medical Perspective."

mal animistic magick, transformation, and awakening to feral power. This is what this book is all about. People have always yearned to unleash the wild and free animal power locked within them, to gain prowess, strength, clarity and a wild joy in living as an integrated part of nature. This magick has been very common throughout human history until the industrial revolution, when it was suppressed. Such magick can be traced all the way back to ancient times and still exists today.

Through study and practice, you can discover ways to shift your consciousness and energetic or etheric body into a human-wolf union, a werewolf. This is possible on several levels: psychologically, energetically, magically, and spiritually.

I hesitate to say physically, but over the last few years I have become more animalistic from these practices in unexpected ways. My night vision became shockingly better. I suddenly got hairier, more than age could account for. My sensitivity to smell became acute. I walked the walk. Join me and we will transform together into something unexpected, marvelous, and free.

Much of what I have discovered has been well known by a variety of earth-centered cultures that recognized the primacy of nature and the spiritual power of wolves and of shape-shifting. I honor and acknowledge all such cultures and accept that their rituals and spirituality are their own. I am grateful for the spiritual examples that they have presented as I have tried to create my own path with werewolf magick.

This book is written mostly for those sympathetic with the beliefs embodied in Animist, Pagan, polytheist, Witchcraft, and other such systems that accept the primacy of nature and the gods, spirits, and magick of nature. Animalistic shape-shifting is rooted in all these traditions and my goal is to help others revive such practices in these communities and traditions. I reference several werewolf gods, goddesses, and spirits in this book, but werewolf magick can work with a variety of spiritual expressions, yours being the key. I support anyone who integrates this work into their particular path. I strongly believe that this is a crucial time to use our spiritual power to help all wild animals and our threatened environment. This is a key ethos and goal of werewolf magick: Gaia is all.

Werewolves, Witchcraft, and Wicca

I take a special joy in providing this work to brothers and sisters in the Craft. Keys to werewolf magick were found in Witchcraft trial documents as well as a few old grimoires. Many accused and real witches died offering clues that I used to re-create this magick. In Europe, werewolves and witches were often entwined, and being accused of one was often grounds for being accused of the other. You will see much in this book that will throw a new light on old Craft practices, like a later chapter on working with Fetches. I believe that anyone interested in old traditional Witchcraft practices will find much in this book to interest and, I hope, excite them.

Shamanism of the Nani Doro or Ulchi People

The key to understanding shape-shifting in the context of werewolf magick lies with ancient practices of what is generally called shamanism. Shamanism is a set of ancient animalistic spiritual practices that were once very common but are less common today. I am not a shaman nor speak for true shamanic tribal cultures, but I have sat with, talked to, and learned from them, My use of the term is thus historical as well as based on my real-life experiences with shamans who referred to themselves as such.

I spent a week in Guatemala with a shaman who was our guide and who took us to a gathering of shamans where the Maya deity named the "smoking god" was venerated. I also learned from the Huichol indigenous culture in Mexico. However, I spent the most time with a group of Siberian shamans who followed the path called Nani Doro. These shamans came to Seattle to present their practices and give workshops in the late 1990s. I was able to interview and take workshops and learned firsthand what shamanism was. I have been very lucky and blessed to meet, listen to, and work with shamans from the Ulch tribe of Siberia, which I met in the mid-1990s.[2] I bow in honor and thanks to these shamans for sharing their wisdom, art, music, and techniques with me, as well as their humor and joy of life. I thank them for putting up with the many foolish questions I asked them about their practices and shape-shifting.

---

2. More information about the Ulch tribe of Siberia and the path of Nani Doro can be found on my website, www.dennysargentauthor.com.

This forms the basis for my use of the term, my concrete experiences with real tribal shamans. I do not claim to be or have expertise in shamanism and am particularly sensitive to and unhappy about the proliferation of the term and the ideas that are generally called shamanism in the new age movement. However, I am referencing the ancient practices and what I know of them because they are at the root of shape-shifting and have informed and inspired my werewolf magick practice. I also want to be clear that I do not claim werewolf magick is shamanism; it borrows ideas and techniques from what I learned from shamans. This encompasses a wide collection of animistic practices that humans have used since we recorded shape-shifting in cave paintings. Spiritual shape-shifting practices, a technique often used in shamanism, still survive today in small indigenous villages.

Learning about the practices from my Maya Guatemalan guide and the Ulchi shamans I interviewed helped me come to my own understanding about what "real" shape-shifting was about. Understanding shape-shifting informed many of my own personal experiences and helped me understand what I was experiencing when werewolf magick emerged later in my life. Their personal animal spirits varied between the cultures. When I learned with the Ulchi, I spoke with their sacred Bear Spirit rather than the Wolf. The Bear Spirit's wisdom, insight, and deep connection with these animal spirits helped guide me in my work. As she said when discussing her ethos and her shamanism to me, "Every step upon the Mother Earth must be one of gratitude." I will never forget this and strive to follow it.

I mention other shamanic cultures like the Huichol— an indigenous culture in Mexico—but it was the Siberian Ulchi I met whom I most honor for spending much time with me and helping me feel the truth about the animal spirits and shape-shifting.

The Animalself

I describe the Animalself as your "inner beast," which many of us have locked away but at what price? You can never be whole without embracing your Animalself. This is the power that drives werewolf magick. The Animalself could also be described with a more psychological explanation: the Animalself is the primordial and instinctual animal part of our psyche or soul, akin to Sigmund Freud's id and Carl Jung's shadow, but it is also embodied in our physical body and genetics. Yes, that is quite a bundle for one concept but we are complicated animals; intellectual but also primal. We are brilliant *Homo sapiens*, but we also share 84 percent of our genetics with canines, which include wolves.[3] It is my opinion from research and practice that the Animalself resides within the deepest part of our unconscious mind, physically in our lower cortex, or "animal brain." This is linked with the group unconscious mind and thus all the archetypal forces and the primal genetic consciousness of all beings we have evolved from. The goal of werewolf magick is to awaken, free, and revitalize our whole being by the energizing and reviving of this part of our brain, our Animalself.

Before you begin this magick, I suggest you learn more about wolves and think deeply about your relationship with the species and upon what your own Animalself may be like. Spend more time in nature, unplug from technology, and feel your true place in the ecosystem as the animal you truly are. As you do so, maybe think on a prayer I make to Gaia daily: *To you, from you: all things.* May this book help you howl with greater joy and awaken to the power and awareness of your true animal being.

---

3. Garrett-Hatfield, "Animals That Share Human DNA Sequences."

CHAPTER 1
HISTORY, LORE AND WEREWOLF CULTS
———————— ╫ ————————

In the shadowy world of myths, legends, and historical sources, we can find the roots of the current practices and beliefs of werewolf magick. To understand this work, it is important to have a mythological and historical background. Knowing that shape-shifting werewolfery has a lineage reaching back to ancient times gives us an understanding of how our ancestors approached and utilized werewolf power and shape-shifting so we may do the same. This history offers us ways to rebuild and reactivate this powerful tradition.

The Beginning

Petroglyphs and pictographs in ancient caves are the earliest indications of human culture and beliefs and some contain images reminiscent of shape-shifting magick.

"Around 30-35,000 years ago there was an explosion of symbolism in paleo-lithic human culture around the world, primarily represented by cave art … Whilst many of the images are naturalistic images of humans, mammals and birds, there is also extensive representation of therianthropic beings, that is part human, part animal shape-shifters."[4]

Among the many such images, werewolf images have been found in ancient cave paintings in the Pyrenees mountains.[5]

---

4. Lewis-Williams, "Shamanic Explorations of Supernatural Realms: Cave Art—The Earliest Folklore."

5. Curran, *Werewolves: A Field Guide to Shapeshifters, Lycanthropes, and Man-beasts*, 19.

Similar shape-shifting images and lore can be found all over the world and werewolves seem to appear wherever wolves roamed. These shape-shifting images are some of humanity's earliest magickal images.

"The neuropsychological and ethnographic evidence that I have adduced strongly suggests that, in these subterranean images, we have an ancient and unusually explicit expression of a complex shamanic experience that is informed by altered states of consciousness."[6]

Shape-shifting practices are likely some of the earliest spiritual practices practiced by our ancestors and are still alive today. It's these practices that are the roots of werewolf magick.

Prehistoric Wolf Powers, Spirits, and Shape-Shifters

We love werewolves but there are many other shape-shifters in legends and myths around the world. I have traveled to Russia, China, and Southeast Asia, where people discussed legends about wer-tigers. In Japan, where I lived for four years, there are numerous tales of kitsune or wer-foxes and of "tanuki" who can appear as human-tanuki or wer-raccoons to steal your food or sake if you wander in the woods at night. Werewolves are seen in popular Japanese culture as "wolf people" and okami or "wolf gods" have shrines dedicated to them that I have visited. When I was in Morocco, I heard about family lines of wer-jackals from my guide. In these countries some people I met believe that such shape-shifting animal-people are actually real and live among them. There was and still is a belief that people have been magickally transforming into a variety of animals since the dawn of time in a number of cultures I have visited. Some of these beings are feared, but many are honored or simply accepted.

There is also a pervasive belief in wolves as divine ancestors. Several royal lineages trace themselves directly back to a wolf ancestor, such as some Turkic tribes and Mongolian royalty. A number of Native American tribes honor a wolf totemic tribal ancestor as well. Viking kings of the past were given titles of being "wolf-born" due to the belief in their shape-shifting abilities.

---

6. Lewis-Williams, "Shamanic Explorations of Supernatural Realms: Cave Art—The Earliest Folklore."

In all of these legendary accounts of werewolves, there are the intertwining threads of the mythic and the magickal, for humans and beasts were and are both animals. It seems it is only relatively recently that we have separated the two.

A Brief History of Werewolf Cults across Cultures

Wherever wolves roamed, there have been werewolf cults that both worshipped the powers of the wolf and claimed knowledge about becoming werewolves. For thousands of years and across many different cultures, these cults were accepted, as was the ability to shape-shift.

We will focus on classical ancient cultures of the Western world and later European cultures that emerged from them. Through this we will see how pervasive the mythos and magick of werewolves was and how those ancient cultures will influence the rituals and spells in our werewolf magick.

Mesopotamia—The First Human-to-Wolf Transformation?

The earliest surviving story of a man-to-wolf transformation can be found in *The Epic of Gilgamesh*, a more than two-thousand-year-old collection of stories from Mesopotamia. Included is a story about a young shepherd who fell deeply in love with the goddess Ishtar. He called on her often and left many offerings at her shrine until she grew bored with his devotions and transformed him into a wolf. It did not end well for him since his own dogs attacked him.[7]

Cults on Mount Lykaion, Greece

According to ancient Greek historians, werewolf cults predated worship of the Hellenic gods. The sacred mountaintop sanctuary on Mount Lykaion in Arcadia, Greece, was likely the oldest center of wolf and werewolf worship in Greece. It was dedicated to a very ancient wolf god thought to have been named Lycaeus ("wolf god," sometimes written as Lykeios). In later Hellenistic times, "Lycaeus" becomes attached to the names of other gods. For example, the god governing the temple changed and became Zeus Lycaeus, another temple nearby honored Pan Lycaeus, and Apollo Lycaeus was worshipped at

---

7. Bettini, "The Rage of the Wolf: Metamorphosis and Identity in Medieval Werewolf Tales."

several other shrines in Greece. In Arcadia, and elsewhere, the cult of this wolf god was widespread. Arcadia hosted the Lycaea festival and games to honor this deity. Both the local city and the festival were said to have been founded by King Lycaon (wolf king) and recent archaeological evidence suggests that human sacrifice and ritual cannibalism were practiced there from prehistoric times. Now we are clearly getting to the werewolfery.[8]

In 380 BCE Plato mentions King Lycaon, as the "protector-turned-tyrant" of the shrine of this wolf-god temple and its werewolf priests. Ovid tells us the full story about Lycaon, who made the mistake of offering Zeus cooked human flesh to test him when he appeared at the temple in human form. According to Ovid, Zeus, being a god, realized what was up, became very angry and turned Lycaon into a werewolf and chased him off. This may be a tale of the cult of Zeus superseding the much older werewolf cult of Lycaeus. In any event, Zeus Lycaeus or "wolfish Zeus" thus became the god of that temple complex, but werewolf stories, human sacrifice, and cannibalism apparently did not end.[9]

The Greek historian Agriopas relates in his journal that the famous athlete Demaenetus assisted at a human sacrifice to Jupiter Lycaeus there, ate of it, and was changed into a werewolf for nine years. He "recovered" and took part in the Olympic games. I can only assume he did well with all that werewolf power and got a medal in something.[10]

The Roman historian Pliny, quoting Evanthes, tells of a related ritual used for becoming a great hunter, which involved going to a nearby sacred lake, leaving your clothes on a tree, swimming across this magickal lake and thus becoming a werewolf. After nine years you would return as a human, with amazing hunting powers. Some interpret this as possibly being a story indicating an initiation into the werewolf cult.[11]

Pausanias, a Greek historian, notes that people who entered the temple of Jupiter Lycaeus "lost their shadow" while in the presence of the wolf god. This

---

8. Franklin, "Chapter 3: The Wolf-Deity in Greece," in *The Lupercalia*, 23.

9. Koosmen, "The Ancient Origins of Werewolves."; Franklin, "Chapter 3—The Wolf-Deity in Greece" in *The Lupercalia*, 21.

10. Koosmen, "The Ancient Origins of Werewolves."

11. Baring-Gould, *The Book of Werewolves*, 10.

fascinating bit of esoteric trivia may have influenced the common European folklore that werewolves cast no shadow. Maybe such werewolves were astral formulations of real werewolf shape-shifters whose astral form would not cast a shadow.[12]

The Cult of Apollo Lycaeus (Wolf Apollo) in Greece

The cult of Apollo Lycaeus spread to many parts of Greece, but it was centered on the Corinthian Isthmus and especially at Argos. It may seem odd that a Sun God like Apollo was associated with wolves, but one of Apollo's original forms was that of a wolf. His mother, Leto, escaped Hera with the help of divine wolves before giving birth to him and his sister Artemis, who is also associated with wolves and werewolves. "Wolf Apollo" was known as a protector of humans in peril and a master of wolves. As such he was invoked to ward off attacking enemies according to Greek historian Aeschylus. As an opponent of evil, he was said to protect herds of livestock like goats and sheep, as well as children. Famous statues of "Wolf Apollo" were erected at Delphi and at his temple in Athens. The Apollo Lycaeus cult also had a temple in conjunction with the werewolf cult of Soranus in Italy.[13]

In Scythia

The Greek historian Herodotus took werewolf cults seriously and on his travels in 425 BCE he wrote about the Neuri. The Neuri were a large nomadic tribe he visited whom he called "magical men." They were living in the land of Scythia, which overlapped parts of what is today Russia. He recounts how the entire tribe changed into werewolves for set periods of time every year:

> It seems that the Neuri are sorcerers, if one is to believe the Scythians and the Greeks established in Scythia; for each Neurian changes himself, once in the year, into the form of a wolf, and he continues in that form

---

12. Pausanias, *Description of Greece*, 27.
13. Summers, *The Werewolf*, 152.

for several days, after which he resumes his former shape (Herodotus Lib. iv. c. 105.).[14]

Here we have not just a small werewolf cult centered on a temple, but a whole clan that turns into werewolves. In the ancient world such wholesale shape-shifting is not unheard of, as you'll see.

Roman Werewolf Cults

Romans were all about wolves and werewolves and the Roman culture that remained after the empire's fall is likely where much of the werewolf lore in Europe originated. For example, the Roman historian Petronius recorded a story of a soldier who agreed to accompany him to Capua at night for protection. Along the way as night fell, the man began to "converse with the stars" and then stripped and suddenly turned into a huge wolf that ran off, leaving poor Petronius shocked and alone. Unsure what to do next, he kept walking until he came to a farmhouse where he chatted with an upset farmer. Just before he had arrived, several farm animals had been killed by a sudden attack of a large wolf. Shaken, the farmer told him that he and his workers had fought off the marauding wolf and had wounded it in the neck with a spear. Petronius finished his travel alone. Returning back to his town the next day, he visited the home of the soldier who had rudely abandoned him, I assume to give him grief, and found that the soldier was in bed *recovering from a bleeding neck wound*. His final statement was "I saw at once that he was a man who could 'change his skin' (versipellis) and never again could I eat bread with him."[15] This is just one of many such Roman werewolf stories.

There was a widespread belief in werewolves or "skin changers" (versipelli) and they were often connected to various werewolf cults, some of which, like the Lupercalia cult, were sanctioned by the state religion of Rome and involved several gods and goddesses.

"The wolf-cults of Italy present the appearance of a religious survival from a remote time. Of an actual wolf-god, we find far fewer manifestations

---

14. Baring-Gould, *The Book of Werewolves*, 8.

15. Baring-Gould, *The Book of Werewolves*, 12.

than in Greece. Yet in the realm of magic, augury, and popular superstition, the wolf was more conspicuous and more highly venerated in Italy than any other animal."[16]

Lupercalia: The Roman "Mother of All Werewolf Festivals"

Roman mythology describes the city of Rome as being founded by Romulus and Remus, who were both allegedly raised by the divine she-wolf Lupa. Rome was named after Romulus and Lupa was always venerated and worshipped there. The great festival of Lupercalia (Wolf Festival) was allegedly in honor of her and of the founding of Rome, though it had actually begun long before the founding of Rome, primarily as a wolf-centered fertility and agrarian festival. It is likely that Lupa was a prehistoric ancient guardian goddess. During the festival of Lupercalia, half-naked "werewolf priests" (Lupercai) ran about the city in scanty goatskins and carrying goatskin cords which they used to whip willing young women who desired help with fertility. The festival was named after Lupercus (wolf god), but the title "Lupercus" seems to have been created as a title for this mysterious wolf god much later. The forest-wolf god being worshipped was generally agreed upon to be Faunus, the Roman version of Pan, who was a much older deity and who is more often described as the shadowy God of Lupercalia. The priests of Faunus were also called Lupercai. Go Romans! In a brief summary, this festival was a debauch for several days with a focus on overt sexuality, fertility, and rampant drinking with werewolf priests howling and running amok, whipping unclad women and I'd guess men as well. Everything in Rome shut down for days, much to the horror of more conservative Romans. What a werewolf party![17]

The final and ironic end of this ancient festival came with the conquest of Christianity. However, so popular was that festival that though the Church tried to end it, they couldn't. As with many popular Pagan festivals, the Church did the next best thing: it co-opted it. In 494 CE, Pope Gelasius I ironically made Lupercalia the Festival of the Purification of the Virgin Mary. Some say

---

16. Franklin, "Chapter 4—The Wolf-Deity in Italy" in *The Lupercalia*, 29.
17. Adkins, *Dictionary of Roman Religion*, 136.; Leach, *Funk & Wagnalls Standard Dictionary of Folklore Mythology and Legend*, 654.

that Valentine's Day, which falls on the same date, was also connected with the "love fest" of Lupercalia. An interesting twist on this licentious and bawdy festival and one that I'm sure made the wolfish Faunus laugh.[18]

The Cult of Soranus and Dis Pater

North of Rome, the god Soranus of Mount Soracte was worshipped by a werewolf cult that was quite famous, even into the Christian era. Their werewolf cult rituals included fire-walking by "man-wolf" priests, a very unusual cult practice in Roman religion, but one that made sense since the area was and still is volcanic. As many classical werewolf cults did, they worked with a chthonic, or underworld, aspect of their wolf god. The site of this cult, Mount Soracte, was wolf-shaped, and the god Soranus was associated with volcanic fire and poisonous vapors. Soranus was considered a chthonic or underworld death god as well, sometimes syncretized with the Roman underworld god Dis Pater. The werewolf cult priests were called Hirpi Sorani with the word "hirpi" meaning wolf in the language of the Sabine people, an ancient culture group that lived just north of Rome before the city's founding.

The cult of Soranus was formed when a pack of wolves stole the meat offerings to Soranus off the temple altar. When angry priests chased them into a volcanic cave, the fumes killed the priests but spared the wolves. Afterward, a strange disease erupted and when the priests sought oracles from their god, the priests were told that they needed to turn into wolves and then the plague would end. Thus, the Soranus cult was founded, the plague ended, and all was well. Many would come yearly to the cult's wolf-god festival to see the sacred fire walking by the entranced werewolf priests of Soranus.[19]

Ares and Mars Werewolf Cults

It is worth noting that werewolf cults were also prevalent in several warrior priesthoods and martial brotherhoods, such as those of Ares and Mars, gods that found wolves to be sacred. Wolf and werewolf symbols were venerated in their temples and worn proudly by these martial cult members and asso-

---

18. Adkins and Adkins, *Dictionary of Roman Religion*, 73 and 136.
19. Adkins and Adkins, *Dictionary of Roman Religion*, 210.

ciated soldiers. The Roman historian Livy wrote about a "statue of Mars on the Appian Way with images of wolves" and Roman poet Horace talks about the Martialis Lupos, the iconic "warrior wolf" symbol often depicted on the standards that were carried into war. The Roman soldiers carried statues of the divine wolf into battle and referred to themselves as "wolves of Mars." The appearance of the wolf of Mars was a sign that Roman victory was to come.[20]

Norse Werewolves

Wolves and werewolves were everywhere in what is now Germany and Scandinavia, as well as Anglo-Saxon-era England, wherever the god Odin (or Woton) was worshipped.

From my reading of the sagas and Norse religious documents it seems that werewolf and bear shape-shifter cults of the Eigi Einhamir or "those not of one skin" or "skin-changers" were accepted in ancient Norse societies and religious traditions. Such shape-changers were seidr (sorcerers) or seidr-assisted warriors who the sagas say could change into man-beasts, most commonly wolf-men or bear-men. This second shape-shifting shape was called their original shape, or "hamr," and the phrase used to indicate the transition of human to werewolf was "skipa homum" or "hamaz." Romping about the countryside in a wolf shape was called "hamfor."[21]

Odin, whose name can be translated into "Master of Ecstasy," was a patron of shape-shifters and very much associated with wolves. It was said that he could fall into a trance of ecstasy and project his soul into the form of another person or animal while appearing to others to be asleep or dead as he traveled forth in various forms. He wore a wolfskin and had two ferocious wolf spirit helpers as his Familiars, Geri and Freki (their names meaning Ravenous and Greedy). The Valkyries, the demigoddesses who carried up the honored warrior dead to Valhalla, rode on his spirit wolves. Much werewolf imagery and mythos comes from Norse religious sagas that survived in Iceland, carried there during the spread of Christianity in the region.[22]

---

20. Häussler, "Wolf Mythology-Italy."
21. Baring-Gould, *The Book of Werewolves*, 8.
22. McCoy, "Odin."

Berserkers were likely the most famous Norse wolf shape-shifters in many ways, and through shape-shifting cult rituals many took on the aspects of bestial and wolfish men, reportedly with huge increases in strength, ferocity, and warrior prowess. Such a wizard-warrior was thus proclaimed a "hamrammr" or wer-bear or werewolf. The hero Harold Harfagr, a legendary Norse mythological hero, is mentioned in sagas as being "in wolfskin" and being of a band of wolfish berserkers or "ulfhe(d)nir," wolf-coated men. The word "berserker" can be traced to warriors wearing "bear-sarks" or bearskins, so technically a werewolf warrior was called an "ulf-sark" but the term berserker became common for all such shape-shifters. In the sagas you will find various heroic warriors named "Ulfhamr," meaning wolf-shaped.[23]

Other Norse werewolf sorcerers transformed themselves through Norse occult rituals and were able to "change skins" as they liked, often for sport, hunting, or robbery. Unlike berserkers, they would simply "put on the wolfskin" and enter full wolf form and go on adventures while their bodies lay comatose in a safe place. This is a very different sort of shape-shifting that was more about leaving the human body behind to enter a new wolf form rather than shifting one's body into a wolfish being. This leaving of the body via one's Double—a sort of soul-like form we will discuss later—and manifesting as a wolf was described by the scholar Sabine Baring-Gould: "…the human body was deserted and the soul entered the second form, leaving the first body in a cataleptic state, to all appearances dead."[24]

Baring-Gould, in his ubiquitous *The Book of Werewolves*, goes on to say that such werewolf sorcerers then went on journeys in their second wolf "hamr," or form, that was "either borrowed or created for this purpose."

It was said that such a werewolf sorcerer was then able to do what a normal human could do but also had the power and skills of a wolf as well. Thus they were considered a true werewolf. When going forth in this manner the sorcerer went on what was called a "wolf's-ride" or "gandrei(d)."[25]

---

23. Baring-Gould, *The Book of Werewolves*, 36.

24. Baring-Gould, *The Book of Werewolves*, 36.

25. Baring-Gould, *The Book of Werewolves*, 17.

Baring-Gould also wrote about another way shape-shifting into a wolf could be accomplished, with a glamour or illusion spell rather than actual transformation. This seems to indicate a different magickal operation, not a transformation but the casting of an illusion through magick. Through incantation it seemed a sorcerer could charm others into seeing them as a wolf or werewolf while they actually remained human. Several of these practices will be referenced in the later chapters in this book on shape-shifting.

In the Norse Völsunga saga, there's a tale of two brothers who chanced upon a cabin where two exhausted werewolf sorcerers were sleeping in human form, their magick wolf pelts hung up. It was "the tenth day that they'd quit their second state," meaning they were recovering from a wolf-journey or shape-shifting romp. The brothers recognized them as sorcerers because, aside from the wolf cloaks, the sleeping pair had "great gold rings on them" (likely ritual torqs) revealing their "dealings with witchcraft," not a negative comment but one of respect. The spying brothers then quietly entered the cabin and stole the hanging wolf pelts. Putting them on they were immediately changed into werewolves and had many wild adventures before cursing their wolf forms and finally finding a way back to being human. They then were compelled to return the robes and were punished by the sleepy sorcerers.[26]

There were other references to similar werewolf transformations, members of various werewolf cults, and lineages in other Norse sagas. There were werewolf cults all across northern Europe and it is no coincidence that the wide range of such werewolf magick corresponded to the wide area where wolves lived. These wolves were symbolic of ferocity, loyalty, power, and protection.

Werewolves in the Celtic World

Wolves and werewolves were often seen in a positive light in the Celtic world. In Ireland, certain tribes in the medieval kingdom of Ossory were reported to become werewolves during Yule, devouring livestock, getting wild, and afterward turning back to human form. Other Irish tribes claimed their ancestors were wolves and often prayed to wolf spirits and wolf gods for help and healing. The members of one Celtic werewolf tribe were rumored to change

---

26. Baring-Gould, *The Book of Werewolves,*38.

into werewolves every seven years and this seems to have been a ritualistic shape-shifting, like the Scythian Neuri.[27] Druids were said to be able to shape-shift into wolves as part of their sorcerous work. These werewolf Druid practices did not die out with the spread of Chrisianity. In Mercia in the tenth century, long after Christianity had come, there was a revival in the teaching of Pagan learning led by two archdruids, one named Werwulf, and the name "spirit-wolf" was given to those who opposed Christianity.[28]

Opponents of Christianity were often called werewolves as the Christian conquest spread into what is now the British Isles. One Pagan opponent, Vereticus, King of Wales, along with his whole tribe, was said to have been "turned into werewolves" by Saint Patrick himself because he refused to convert.[29]

Wolves were often connected to royalty. The legendary Irish king Cormac mac Airt of Ireland was supposedly raised by a she-wolf. The wolf was often given a positive role as a helper or a guide in many Irish and Welsh myths. In Scotland, wulvers—creatures with human bodies and wolf heads—were sweet and didn't eat or hurt people, but instead helped lost travelers and left fresh fish they caught for people as gifts.[30] Such nice werewolves! Warriors who fought for various Celtic kings were sometimes praised as werewolves. Celtic culture spread so far that digging deeply would take an entire book, but the idea of shifting into werewolves was seen as a cool skill and generally positive. There were several Celtic gods associated with wolves and werewolves, such as the goddess Morrigan, who sometimes took the form of a wolf, and two gods who are both depicted with wolves, Cernunnos and Sucellus.[31]

Witchcraft and Witch Cults in Medieval Europe

What was called Witchcraft in early Christian Europe was often identified as Satanism by the clergy of the new religion and was often linked with werewolves and shape-shifting, all said by the Church to be the work of

---

27. Walker, *The Woman's Dictionary of Symbols and Sacred Objects*, 282.

28. Walker, *The Woman's Encyclopedia of Myths and Secrets*, 1069.

29. Steiger, *The Werewolf Book: Encyclopedia of Shapeshifting Beings*, 221.

30. Oberon, *A Wizard's Bestiary*, 102

31. Häussler, "Wolf-Mythology-Celtic."

demons. From historical records and research of the survival of Pagan traditions and lore, we know there were certainly some festivals and folklore that continued the "old ways." Surviving Pagans in newly Christianized Europe left few if any verifiable records, but we do have the records of the Christian conquerers who confronted and suppressed surviving Pagan religious traditions. Because of the "heathen" nature of such devilish practices as shape-shifting, the Church set out to eliminate them. In medieval church documents werewolfism and Witchcraft were closely linked. Here is an example from a trial in the sixteenth century:"The fate of Peter Stubbe, a German man, was not so fortunate. After flat-out confessing to having made a deal with the devil, in which Stubbe was gifted a belt allowing him to shape-shift for the sake of killing and consuming countless victims over twenty-five years, he was publicly executed in 1589."[32]

Such persecutions resulted in voluminous records from trials and essays by clerics, which are somewhat horrific documents full of many references to werewolfery. Some of those on trial were insistent that, though they were indeed werewolves, they acted to protect and help humanity for god. During his trial, a self-admitted sorcerer named Thiess insisted that werewolves were not evil but were working for good against the devil as "wolves of god." He testified that he would leave his body in werewolf form and journey to Hell to steal back grain and other precious things that the devils of Hell and evil witches had stolen. As "hounds" or "wolves" of god, they defended society by shedding human skin and taking up the spirit bodies of wolves to go save such magickal things as "luck" and "good crops" for the good of the whole community. They saw themselves as spiritual wolf warriors.[33]

The more common Witchcraft trial transcripts are filled with litanies of satanic sins elicited from poor, tortured peasants who were then executed. Reading these, you realize that the populace and inquisitors all deeply believed in the existence of witches, demons, and werewolf cults. The question still remains: Did surviving remnants of shape-shifting werewolf cults still exist? I believe there is enough evidence to say yes and in the mind of the Church,

---

32. Baring-Gould, *The Book of Werewolves*, 8.
33. Lecouteux, *Witches, Werewolves and Fairies*, 168–174.

there were a lot of them. Olaus Magnus, a cleric of the Church involved in such trials, wrote the following:

> On the feast of the Nativity of Christ, at night a multitude of werewolves gather at a certain spot then spread to attack animals and humans, they eat livestock, [and] drink beer in taverns they raid ... [34]

There are many accounts like this, but amidst the Satanic panic, there were tales that showed a surprising tolerance of werewolves. One story shows they had a helpful side. A nobleman was traveling in Lithuania with others when he ran out of daylight and had to camp deep in the woods without food. One of the servants revealed that he was a werewolf, transformed in the woods out of sight, and returned as a wolf with a sheep in his jaws to feed them all. He then went back into the woods and emerged as a man again. One assumes they all ate well and forgave the werewolf for his affliction. Really, that would be the most awesome friend to have.[35]

The Church declared that werewolfism was forbidden in 1023 CE but had been declared a great evil earlier than that.[36] During the Middle Ages, werewolfery increasingly became a focus of the inquisition and up through the 1700s. It was not uncommon to see such beliefs still discussed. The writer Rhanaeus in the 1700s, who had been studying much older witchcraft trial scripts, shared his research on werewolfery and shape-shifting: "They imagine in deep sleep or dream that they injure the cattle, and this without leaving their couch."[37] As you'll later see, this type of trance shape-shifting indicates that their astral body—also called a Double—was used.

Another important piece of the puzzle pulled out of these witchcraft trial documents has to do with the Lord of the Forest—sometimes also called the Dark Man of the Woods or the Lord of the Woods—who offered power to witches seeking initiation into witchcraft and werewolfery. The interrogators

---

34. Baring-Gould, *The Book of Werewolves*, 53.

35. Baring-Gould, *The Book of Werewolves*, 55.

36. Baring-Gould, *The Book of Werewolves*, 57.

37. Baring-Gould, *The Book of Werewolves*, 60.

forced those being tortured to agree that this mysterious figure was the devil, but that is not always what the accused originally said. The mysterious and powerful Lord of the Forest in these documents would often test those seeking initiation, mark them with a claw or sharp fingernail, then, after some sort of ritual, give the new witch a magickal wolfskin or wolfskin belt along with a special werewolf salve to rub on the body. Rubbing their bodies with the salve and wearing the skin or belt together would turn them into werewolves and the Lord of the Forest would then teach the new witches how to shape-shift. Even though these tales were recounted during torture many of them were fairly consistent with the details.

In 1521 an inquisitor named Boin elicited a confession from an alleged witch and werewolf in rural France. The alleged witch had been in the forest seeking lost sheep when he was approached by a black horseman who asked if he needed help. The man seeking the sheep told the black horseman his story and the black horseman then offered to help the shepard find his sheep and give him money. They met in the forest days later at an agreed-upon time and place and to the shepard's surprise his sheep were there and the black horseman gave him money. He was so happy he agreed to follow the black horseman, which turned out to be the Lord of the Forest. At their next meeting, the aspirant renounced Christianity and agreed to bind himself to the Lord of the Forest, whom he later identified while being tortured as the devil. They met again in the woods and this time many other witch cult initiates were present. This alleged witch described in his testimony that they all danced a special dance with green tapers burning blue flames, stripped and rubbed a special salve on their bodies, and were quickly changed into wolves.[38]

There is one specific part of the story that I believe indicates shape-shifting was involved: The alleged witch noted in his testimony that he was horrified at his four wolf feet and the fur that he was covered with, but he found that he could travel with the "speed of wind," something modern shape-shifters also describe about spirit travels.

---

38. Baring-Gould, *The Book of Werewolves*, 70.

Though this transformation was done with the help of the Lord of the Forest, this alleged witch said he couldn't perceive the Lord of the Forest until he returned to human form. This seems to indicate an awakening from a spirit journey because he would have had the sight of a wolf which is far less accurate than that of a human.

The salve used for shape-shifting is often mentioned in such witchcraft trial documents as being used to fly to the sabbat as well as for changing into wolves. Most likely the salve was a psychotropic trigger substance full of herbal drugs such as belladonna and aconite for launching one into spirit journeys. Many modern shape-shifters describe feeling exhausted after such "journeys," and a number of trial transcripts talk about werewolves being exhausted for days and often laid up in bed after such astral adventures. This exhaustion is much the same as that experienced by the Norse sorcerers mentioned previously.

Witches were also said to ride to the sabbat on the back of werewolves. One could assume these were devilish pals of theirs but, as you'll see later in the book, they also could have been their Fetches—spiritual beings created from one's own energy. It was amazingly common for witches to be accused of werewolfism of all kinds. This may indicate that the surviving Pagan witches could have been influenced or remnants of pre-Christian shape-shifting practices as described in the ancient werewolf cults. So many other Roman festivals and folk beliefs endured in Europe at this time that it certainly seems possible.

To show how similar these werewolf and witchcraft patterns are, it is important to add testimony from a very well-known witchcraft trial, that of Jean Grenier. We can skip all the horrific propaganda about him devouring children and so on, but how he entered a "werewolf cult" in the 1600s is interesting and is similar to many other accounts. Here are his words:

> When I was ten or eleven years old, my neighbor Duthillaire introduced me to the depths of the forest, to the 'Master of the Forest,' a black man, who signed me with a nail and then gave me and him a salve and a wolf skin. From that time I have run about the country as a wolf. [39]

---

39. Baring-Gould, *The Book of Werewolves*, 92.

Grenier accused his father of inducting him into the cult, which makes sense because much werewolf lore includes descriptions of tribal, clan, bloodline, or family connections in werewolf cults. Grenier said his father also had a magickal wolfskin and occasionally accompanied him as a wolf.

Summation of Werewolf History

In this chapter, we have seen how shape-shifting practices spread and changed throughout history. We started in the ancient world, then tracked them from the fall of the Roman Empire into Europe where it seems that some werewolf cult practices continued surviving despite efforts by the spread of Christianity to eradicate Pagan practices like shape-shifting as "evil." Knowing all this helps create a framework for understanding werewolf magick today. We are now ready to see how we can reconstruct and revive these practices through creative exercises, spells, and rituals rooted in historical research combined with inspiration and real practice. That being said, let's growl, howl, and leap into the work.

CHAPTER 2
PRINCIPLES OF WEREWOLF MAGICK

———————— ⵑⵑ ————————

K nowing where we have been as werewolf cult fans helps us see where we are going in this modern era with werewolf magick. We will now explore werewolf magick as a neo-traditional practical system of shape-shifting magick that can aid us in connecting with our Animalself, a part of us we have ignored. Our goal in working on this magick is to increase joy, pleasure, and self confidence, and create a powerful connection with nature. Exploring the ancient folklore of how to become a werewolf inspires and informs the fundamental concepts, ideas, and symbols of this revived werewolf magick. All of this will prepare us for the real meat of werewolf magick, shape-shifting, and actively practicing the rites and spells of werewolf magick.

The Term "Werewolf"

We have already learned that the ancient Norse used the magickal term "wer-wulf" for "one who wore the skin of a wolf." The term entered old English and high German as "wer-wulf" and then werewolf. In old Normandy the term was "garwaf," in old French it was "garwall," "guaroul," or "garu." You've heard the term Loup Garou, loup being "wolf." Much of these terms came from the Low Latin term for werewolf, "gerulphus."[40]

This dip into linguistics is to make the point that most people in the Western world, until the modern era, had serious terms for things we would consider fanciful. It is unusual for cultures to have terms that are not part of their

———————————————————

40. Jackson, *The Compleat Vampyre: The Vampyre Shaman, Werewolves, Witchery & the Dark Mythology of the Undead*, 61.

cultural schema, so terms like spirits or elves or ghosts are almost always, in my experience as a historian and linguist, rooted in some form of belief. We know that even up to the 1700s the Church issued proclamations stating that werewolves and witches were quite real and doing Satan's work. Therefore it stands to reason that pre-Christian cultures that used the various terms for werewolves believed in them. Looking at the records of ancient historians like Herodotus and writers of the Norse sagas, it is clear that werewolves were a very real thing to people, from ancient times until the 1800s, and still are today for some. Such wolfish shape-shifting still exists amongst the Huichol shamans in Mexico, giving another example of shape-shifting werewolf practices happening today.

The Reality of Transforming into a Werewolf

The myth of transforming into a werewolf is that you become a real creature that involves a painful physical change of the flesh and bones, into the form of a wolf. This curse of transformation comes from being bitten by a werewolf or is acquired from sorcery or a demon. This actual bone and flesh ripping physical transformation is, as far as I know, a fantasy.

The transformations we will be working on in werewolf magick aren't violent. Through intense physical, meditative, magickal, and physiological actions one calls forth the deepest primal part of the unconscious mind—the Animalself—in the form of a wolf spirit. This is aided by accessing the 84 percent of genetic material shared between humans and canines. Shape-shifting is done by focusing and directing the Animalself to psychologically, spiritually, and physically come forth so one can manifest or "wear" the astral form of the Animalself in the form of a werewolf. This was what the Norse called "wearing the wolf or true skin." As we will see, werewolf magick and shape-shifting can be done by calling up or *evoking* our wolf-power from within and by *invoking* or calling to us external, divine natural forces to aid us, all embodied as gods and goddesses. As without, so within; as within, so without. The spiritual and energetic work we do within our mind and body manifests in our outer reality. This often-referenced saying in magick is the underlying thesis of this werewolf transformation and as the stories of berserkers show, has some validity. Mind over matter is a real thing in my experience, and having seen real possessions, fire walking, and apparent ritual transformation with my own eyes, I believe it is real.

From my studies and experiences, I believe that werewolf magick is best effected by a combination of evoking and invoking wolf-power through the activation of the Animalself with the end result being shape-shifting.

Remember, humans have been doing this since ancient times and still do. Every human being can accomplish astounding physical, spiritual, and mental feats when they have belief, energy, focus, and will. This includes healing their physical body, reformulating their psyche, and altering the way they appear to others.

The Double

A common belief among shape-shifters is a belief in an astral body that is separate from a soul, a belief that was common in many ancient cultures such as the Greeks, Egyptians, and Vikings, and continues to be believed today. This astral body is energetic in nature and with will and magick, can leave or empower the physical body. By placing oneself into a deep, energized trance, often with divine help from the natural energy invoked as spirits or gods, a magickian can empower, shape, and use this astral body, what we'll be calling a Double.[41]

One way to do this is to evoke the primal power of the Animalself in a chosen animal form, a wolf for example. Consciousness is then extended into this astral wolf form through the will of the magickian and can rise up within the magickian or become a separate spiritual entity. This is done when the magickian places some or all of their consciousness into that astral wolf form. Once the astral body has been consciously shaped and filled with the person's consciousness, it can be used in two ways:

1. The magickian, in a trance, can send it forth with their consciousness to travel about this world or other spirit worlds at will by becoming the actual astral body—or Double—that is invoked and evoked and into

---

41. Lecouteux, *Witches, Werewolves, and Fairies*, xiii.

which one's consciousness then abides. Thus, one becomes the Double, which can be used for spirit travel. Some of the examples we have already learned about from the previous chapter include shape-shifters using this Double to travel to the underworld and Norse shape-shifters leaving their entranced body to roam about as wolves.

2. Do what the Norse seidr called "wearing the wolf skin," and physically call up the wolf power from within and then ride this astral spirit or Double. The Double, or Wolf Spirit, is then ridden by the consciousness of the magickian to go forth, much as witches were said to "ride the werewolf" to sabbats. This description is similar to what Ulchi shamans described to me in terms of riding the animal spirit to the spirit world.

Now that we have seen how historical practices of werewolf magick are still used today in connecting with the astral body, we can see how that is the first basic skill to understanding werewolf magick. What follows will help us understand the philosophical, spiritual, and pragmatic ideas, tools, and practices in our hands-on work of mastering the practices of werewolf magick on every level. Like all systems of magick, werewolf magick is guided by a philosophy, ethos, and vision of the spiritual and physical world, as we will see. Ours just happens to have a rather primal, earthy, and wolfish point of view. How fun is that?

Caveats about Werewolf Magick

In terms of practice, this book is primarily aimed at adults due to the contents of some of the exercises and rituals. Unleashing your Animalself is a serious and intense undertaking. Beyond that limitation, all are invited to read and enjoy this book, as werewolf magick is fitting for all types of magickal folks.

Where, When, and How to Do Werewolf Magick

Most of the rituals, exercises, and spells in this book call for doing this work outside in wilderness areas because connecting with the Animalself is all about reconnecting with the primal part of yourself and with nature, things it seems our culture has lost. However, that may not always be possible and that is fine. The key is to reconnect with nature any way you can when doing werewolf work. Adapt! If you live in an urban area, use your local parks. If you have a yard, that will work as well. If you live in an area with few or no trees, any wild or natural place will work, including a beach or desert. If you really need to do this work inside, then get some indoor plants or a small indoor tree.

While many of the rituals intend on werewolf magick being done outside in the wilderness, at night, and often on a full moon, this may not be practical, safe, or easy for you to do. While the full moon is the strongest time to do such work, werewolf magick can be done any time of day that works and is safe for you.

Most werewolf magick work calls for growling, howling, and being wild because, well, werewolves right? Some of the work also calls for burning herbs, lighting candles, and so on. Howling and burning things in a public park won't end well, so flexibility is key. Adapt. For example, if you are going to do some work in a park or yard, you can growl and howl very softly and you can use lavender oil instead of burning lavender. It is the focus, intent, and energy that are most important. Part of werewolf magick is wild freedom and doing things based on instinct, intuition, and insight. If your instinct tells you to do or not do something, listen to it! Your Animalself knows what to do. This book is just a set of guidelines; you are your own wolf!

Nudity and Safety

Werewolf magick seeks to return us to our most primal Animalself; thus the optimal ritual state for all such ritual work and shape-shifting is nakedness. However, it's not necessary and nudity in the wrong place can get you in trouble and can be an issue of safety. While such "sky clad" werewolf magick can be done within one's home or private backyard, it is perfectly acceptable to do any werewolf magick wearing loose, relaxed natural clothing, especially in a wilderness setting. Having your bare feet on the earth can connect you with the earth just fine. It is also perfectly acceptable to bring a friend or two with you for safety into any woods; they can sit and meditate while you do your ritual work or even join in if they desire. You cannot enter a state of freedom and wild joy if you are worried. Adapt any of the ritual work as you need to create a safe space for yourself so your wolf can emerge in freedom.

Drinking

The ritual use of wine, liquor, and beer is mentioned in several rites and rituals in this book. I am following traditional ideas and information. If you do not drink, simply substitute as you need. Fresh fruit juice works fine. Use your intuitive judgment.

Using Meat

Raw or cooked meat is involved in some of the rites and rituals, which are also based off traditional and historical practices. I mean, werewolves, right? Wolves are carnivorous, but they are also omnivores, so if meat isn't your thing, there are other options. Wolves eat berries, fish, and various herbs and vegetables, so there are lots of options, but try to keep it germane to wolves. No tofu, for example. I've made suggestions along the way.

Entheogens

In the previous chapter on the history of werewolf magick, some traditions were thought to use entheogens for werewolf magick. Terence McKenna—an ethnobotanist and proponent for therapeutic psychedelics use—has studied the long history of the practice of using psychedelics or entheogens in trance and shape-shifting work. Some of his work mentions the same practices we learned about in the previous chapter. Shape-shifters and werewolf cults throughout the ages have traditionally utilized a number of entheogens in such magick. More on the topic can be read in McKenna's book *Ethnobotany of Shamanism*. However, for our concerns the use of illegal entheogens is not in any way recommended in the rituals and spells of this book.

The Use of Body Fluids in Rituals

Natural products of the human body such as spit, sexual fluids, and blood have been used in rituals since ancient times, especially in nature-based Pagan or Animist religions. This is a book about animalistic magick. To open up the most primordial consciousness, it is the body that is the primary tool. Using blood, spit, semen, menstrual blood and so on was the norm in ancient Pagan religions and cults. Our work is about consciously decivilizing ourselves in order to reconnect and reclaim our Animalself. This means using and getting attuned with our body and occasionally using these body fluids. We use only natural things in our work, such as leaves, herbs, flowers, spring water, and natural secretions and parts of our bodies. These parts of our bodies include the genetic information that we share with other animals. If blood and sexual fluids are beyond the pale for you, one substitute is spit. However, to avoid the risk of spreading communicable diseases, it is imperative that work with these fluids be immaculate and never shared.

On Sex

In a number of rituals the option to include "self-love" within the working is offered, and actually self-love could be added to any werewolf magick work. This is up to you. Sex magick is very powerful, even more so in werewolf magick because the goal is the eclipsing of the ego by the primordial Animalself and nothing does that faster and more deeply than an orgasm. Sexual ritual work in werewolf magick is generally solo work. You're unleashing your primordial werewolf self; this is your own wolf work.

Werewolves, Tribalism, and Politics

Werewolf magick is individualistic and primordial; the social norms used in this magick are those of the animal world, not the human world. Creating a healthy environment is crucial to werewolf magick practitioners and we aim for a spiritual return to a more primal, integrated consciousness that makes all humans and animals coequal. Wolves, and other animals in nature, do not discriminate when it comes to fur color or sexuality. Werewolf magick in this regard consistently espouses tolerance on all levels. Those who practice this magick are accepting of all with a wild heart, regardless of what color their fur is, their sexuality, or their beliefs, *as long as those beliefs do not include intolerance.* Hate groups, like Nazis, sometimes use terms like "wolf'" and "werewolf" to describe themselves and their hateful ideology. Such beliefs are not in line with real werewolf magick and are not reflected in the animal kingdom.

Final Caveat

I encourage everyone to read, enjoy this book, and only use the rituals or spells they are comfortable with. If some of the more radical paths of werewolf magick are not right for you now, that is fine, but even reading this book or utilizing parts of it will subtly open up a window to your Animalself. Let it open in the way that works for you. No matter what, I encourage you to get out into nature as much as you can.

Key Werewolf Magick Terms Used in This Book

I would argue that this section is one of the most important in the book because it contains many of the terms used in werewolf magick. It is strongly suggested that the following section be carefully read so that a clear understanding of the realities behind werewolf magick may be understood. There are some terms that are used in this book that have very specific meanings in werewolf magick and are used in a very specific way within our work.

Wer: The term wer is used in this book to indicate that a person who is practicing werewolf magick has entered a werewolf shifting trance state. When they are in this state, they are no longer simply human but have mentally and energetically shifted to a werewolf state.

Shape-shifting: This is the practice of moving into a primal mental and energetic animal state. A practitioner will open up to the deep unconscious Animalself, enter a deep trance state, and suppress the conscious mind and ego. In this way we remember our true animal nature and directly empower our instincts, intuition, and insights. Real shape-shifting is complex in practice.

Liminal state: A liminal state indicates a shadowy twilight place between worlds or states of consciousness. The semiconscious state between sleep and wakefulness is called a liminal state, for example. This term is used often in werewolf magick because it is in the mental and spiritual liminal states where the werewolf shifting occurs and where the Double operates. Traditionally, werewolf magick is all about liminal states as you'll see, including between living and death, day and night, myth and reality, and physical and astral. In many cultures which practice similar shape-shifting, a large part of sacred dances, rituals, and magick occur in such liminal states.

Double: Many cultures across the ages have considered the soul to have been made of several parts. One is an eternal spirit, the other is an astral body. The historian Claude Lecouteux in his brilliant book *Witches, Werewolves, and Fairies* refers to this astral body as the Double, as will I. He traces the concept back to ancient Greek theurgy and philosophy. This Double can leave the body to do magick or explore dreams or other dimensions. It is this Double that shape-shifters use to travel to the spirit world. The Double is said to be born with you and fades or transitions when you die, unlike the eternal soul. With training, this Double can be shaped into a specific form to be used in your astral work as a wolf or werewolf. In traditional witchcraft, what we call a Double is often called a Fetch, however later in the book, we will be using the term Fetch for a slightly different use in our werewolf magick.

Types of Werewolf Magick Work

Practices and exercises: These are ritualistic activities that are done with few to no tools and can be done a number of times. Some may be part of longer ritual work.

Rituals: These require more time, effort, and usually the use of various tools and items. Rituals have a clear beginning and ending and often include honoring spirits and gods or goddesses.

Rites: These are shorter, less complex rituals.

Spells: These are usually used for a specific purpose or problem and have a clear goal.

The Gods and Goddesses of Werewolf Magick

We have seen that wolf and werewolf gods and their followers can be found in many different cultures and mythologies. Many have been introduced in our previous chapter, but with a little research you'll find many more. Here are some of the wolf or werewolf cult gods and goddesses we have already learned about: Lycaeus, Zeus Lycaeus, Pan Lycaeus, Apollo Lycaeus, Lupa, Lupercus, Faunus, Soranus, Dis Pater, Ares, Mars, Odin (or Woton), Morrigan, Cernunnos, Sucellos, and the Lord of the Forest.

We honor all of them in werewolf magick and all are worth investigating as deities to work with in werewolf magick rituals. However, there are a few gods and goddesses that you will see repeatedly in the werewolf magick rituals, practices, and spells.

Werewolf magick as it is presented in this book uses a specific set of gods and goddesses. These deities made themselves known as the work of this book evolved and as the magick manifested. Many of us have had such experiences in magick where the right god, goddess, or spirit simply comes when they are needed. As the shaman Nadyezhda Duvan, Wisdom Keeper of the Ulchi, said to me, "You don't choose the spirits, the spirits choose you."[42]

The Lord of the Forest

The Lord of the Forest is a name that has been given to many feral Pagan deities throughout history, often associated with animals, hunting, fertility, primal forests, and untamed nature. This god is animalistic, primal, ferocious, and often depicted with many animals and animal attributes, such as horns and hoofs. Often this god is honored as a guide or lord of the dead as well. Some of the gods that have been called Lord of the Forest or shared similar characteristics include Pan, Cernunnos, Hern, Pashupati, Anu, Faunus, the Green Man, Esus, and Sylvanus, just to name a few. In werewolf magick, the Lord of the Forest is the spirit of wildness and wilderness, protector of the animals, and embodies active representation and manifestation of Gaia. Through him we learn and partake in the wildness and, as werewolves, he is our lord and protector in the wilderness, teaching us the way of being animal.

The Moon Goddess

As the moon is eternally changing, the Moon Goddess—mother, sister, teacher, and sorceress—is all things to us who are werewolves. She embodies our magick and shows us the sacred mysteries of the vast web of power and karma and causality that is our magickal work, the silver spider's web that interconnects all things. She is the teacher of liminal states, trance work, shapeshifting and spellcraft. In this book, three goddesses represent her different

---

42. Sargent, "Nani Doro, The Way of the Siberian Ulchi Shaman."

aspects, but all are one divinity, one lunar goddess power that makes werewolf magick, shape-shifting, and all transformations possible. We honor her with three names which have been linked in myth:

As the dark moon, we call her Hekate. She is mistress of the darkness, sorcery, the crossroads and is often accompanied by and associated with wolves. Sometimes she is shown with three wolf heads and some historians connect her with Cerberus, guardian of the underworld who has three canine heads, which seems right in that she is also a guide and helper of the dead. She is more ancient than most goddesses and all-powerful.

As the full moon, we call her Selene. For werewolves, Selene is the almost overwhelming power of the full moon, the powerful astral influence and gateway of werewolf magick, transformation, and animalistic power. Mistress of all watery tides, including within our bodies, she offers the "lunacy" that fills us all every full moon. It has of course been noted that wolves are prone to howling at her full silvery orb, as are people. The link between full moons and werewolves is about astral work, magick, shape-shifting, and dreams, which is why we love them.

As the crescent moon, we call her Artemis. She is the original "woman who runs with the wolves," and as a youthful huntress is accompanied by Pan's wild dogs, though her dogs are sometimes identified as wolves. She and her brother, Apollo, are both linked with wolf-power and she is called mistress of wild creatures. She was also known as Artemis Lykaina, Artemis the "she-wolf." She is the protector of women and children and aids in childbirth. Artemis has been referenced as a goddess of shape-shifting. One night she found a man named Actaeon spying on her and used her power to transform him into a stag, whom she then hunted down with her dogs, killing him with "the frenzy of a wolf." She is a wild one and we werewolves love her.[43]

Gaia

We call the Earth Mother Gaia, as do many. A simple prayer we often say to Gaia is "to you, from you; all things," for this is the truth. Everything we have is from Gaia. We all love, venerate, and give honor to Gaia, for she is all things

---

43. Häussler, "WolfMythology-Greek."

in werewolf magick and the source of all things. Gaia is used as her title in our magick, but she has many names in every language and all of them call her mother. As wild beings, we come from her, live within her, and subsist on what she gives us. This is truth. As werewolves Gaia is our mother, her forests are our homes, all her creatures are our brothers and sisters. It is that simple. The best we can do is honor Gaia, her wild children, and do our very best to save the environment she has blessed us with.

The Wolf Spirit

It is impossible to really clearly describe or speak of the Wolf Spirit.

The Wolf Spirit, we can suppose, is a great spirit of primal nature which takes the form of a wolf, but what this really means is hard for our human minds to grasp. But once we shape-shift and this spirit fills us and we become a werewolf, it may become clear and obvious! Without the Wolf Spirit, there would be no werewolf magick. We could use terms like egregore or collective spiritual energy but such things are just words. If we go into the wilderness and call to the Wolf Spirit with an open heart and an awakened Animalself, the Wolf Spirit may come to us. May it be so.

There are other spells and rites in this book that call upon other deities, but they can all be seen as aspects of the primal powers of nature. The names are less important than the truth behind the powers. Wolves and other beasts do not name things, they exist with them in the way of life. This is a profound truth.

The Wildness, Wyrd, and Way: The Werewolf Magick Cosmos

All spiritual systems have a schema or framework within which to understand that spiritual worldview. Werewolf magick is a spiritual and magickal system and the Wildness, Wyrd, and Way are the schema of that system, the underlying principles. Without a deep instinctual and intuitive understanding of these three aspects of the werewolf magick worldview, you can not understand the principles that underly this primordial magick. As indicated by the personal and primal aspects of werewolf magick, these principles are not easy to define, though we will seek to understand what they mean and how they work within this magickal system. We should meditate on each of these principles and reality frames deeply since they inform and help manifest everything important about this magickal path.

Wildness

Before all things, the Wildness is sacred in werewolf magick. All things come from and return to Gaia, which includes the Wildness. The Wildness is both the easiest power to grasp and the hardest to explain, but this gnosis power rises within us every time we enter a forest, climb amidst mountains, or wander a deserted wilderness coast. When you camp out, go hiking, or appreciate any primal aspects of nature, we are in Wildness. It is the inherit spiritual, energetic, and living force that is primal nature and the flowing energetic source of all nature. When we sit in any healthy ecosystem, like a deep forest, pause, breathe, and open our whole physical and spiritual self to the experience, we will touch the Wildness on a deep level and are left with a feeling of euphoria and well-being.

Once, eons ago, most of the planet was awash in Wildness and this feeling was our natural state. The few hominids roaming the earth were living within the all-embracing planetary weave of a vast quilt of ecosystems that covered the planet. The key energizing of werewolf magick comes from this power, magick, and elixir of life that is embodied in direct spiritual and physical immersion in Wildness. Werewolf magick encourages each of us to go out into the wilderness as we can and evoke our Animalself and *remember that this is our true home!* It is only through direct physical and spiritual relinking with fountains of Gaia power as an animal, free of human filters and restrictions, that we can truly become the Wildness and so, if we choose, become a werewolf.

Wyrd

Just as the Wildness is the purest primal power, the Wyrd is the weft and web of causality, fate, karma, and the vast interconnections and links within which we weave our lives. The Wyrd is embodied in every ecosystem. Visualize the vast, ever-shifting web of interrelationships, causality, and communication that flows through time and space, matter and energy in that ecosystem. An ecosystem is so complex that even scientists can't comprehend all the variables nor really predict its shifting. Now, visualize our whole existence as a spiritual and physical ecosystem, a vast weave of ever-shifting patterns interwoven within the Wildness. This is the Wyrd. The word Wyrd has been translated in many ways, but the ideas of fate, personal destiny, and/or the weaving of all things comes close. The Wyrd is the matrix within which we live and work with power in our werewolf magick. In fact, the term magick is itself a fair definition of Wyrd. The belief in human exceptionalism has cut us off from the Wyrd, our vital interface with Gaia, and this link must be recovered if our species is to survive.

Way

The Way is beyond intellectual conception or words, which makes it so difficult to explain. The best analogy may be the Chinese philosophy of Tao.

In Japan this ephemeral state is called Wa, a term that does not translate, but is sometimes described with words like totality, harmony, or peace to describe this ego-free consciousness. Way is an English equivalent. It is akin to those moments of pure absence when the wall between self and other vanishes and all reality and sense of self evaporates. It is to truly *be* without ego or sense of self. Animals operate in Way all the time by their very existence, instinctively and playfully living and doing what it is they were made to do. Fish do not "know" when to spawn, birds do not "know" when to migrate and wolves do not "know" how to behave in a pack. It is just part of the Way. If we let go of everything except pure existing while in wild nature, we experience moments of Way. The goal of werewolf magick is to transcend the false dichotomy of beast and human or self and other through immersion in the pure natural state of Way. In this state of pure being we awaken to the animals we are, and so simply are.

These three magickal aspects of werewolf magick, woven together, result in the three core powers that guide those who practice werewolf magick: Instinct, Intuition, and Insight.

Instinct, Intuition, and Insight:
The Powers of the Werewolf

As Wildness, Wyrd, and Way are the three underlying principles of the external werewolf magick universe, so the three powers of werewolf magick define and express the internal powers that are cultivated and honed within the werewolf magickian.

These three powers of werewolf magick are manifested by the werewolf by interacting with the principles of nature in ritual work.

Instinct is the deepest, most primal animal-mind or unconscious knowing. It is something you don't need to learn like we learn rules; it comes naturally. For example, babies cry by instinct, and wolf cubs follow their mother by instinct. It is a genetically hardwired, species-wide unconscious understanding and doing. It is connected with somatic or body memory present in every living animal at birth, including us. We have lost touch with our animal instincts, and werewolf magick will both enhance and expand such instincts. With such expanded animal instincts we can "know" so much without conscious thinking.

Intuition arises from the liminal, emotive state of transitional-consciousness. That is, in our work, from the awakening Animalself and the self-emergent state of more open awareness. This state of consciousness is the place where animals "feel" the truth about things experienced without "knowing" why and so do we. It springs as a certainty in the place where the self and shadow meet and intertwine, offering nonintellectual "gut feelings" drawn from the deepest and highest states of being. When a dog wags its tail at a stranger, it is doing so by intuiting what kind of person they are. We use intuition, for example, when we choose to avoid a certain room because it has "bad vibes."

Unlike Instinct, we use Intuition when we quiet the ego and the higher cortex cognition and feel with our "gut" or animal mind, but in an aware state. By embracing the Animalself and opening up to the increased interconnection with the conscious and unconscious mind our Intuition blossoms.

Insight becomes available to us when our Animalself emerges from the unconscious mind fully into human consciousness. Instinct triggers intuitive gnosis and Intuition unconscious knowing, but Insights arrive like lightning bolts of gestalt understanding. This electric communication between our

Animalself (what Jung calls the shadow) and our higher consciousness (what Jung calls the self) takes the form of deep spontaneous insights that arise spontaneously in the conscious mind like flashes of truth. Insights are not born from reasoning and intellect, nor are they formed from Intuition or Instinct. They are "aha" moments that arise from deep unconscious alchemies and are known as "true and right" immediately, even though they may seem at times illogical or crazy. Scientists and artists often describe entering liminal states which allow deep insights to arise that offer new ways of seeing things but they are unbidden. The werewolf magickian can cultivate this skill though practice.

The Alchemy of Instinct, Intuition, and Insight

Empowering, expanding, and balancing Instinct, Intuition, and Insight are the key practices of werewolf magick on a daily basis. Skill at this helps us remain rational while at the same time being immersed in the sensory tsunami of the Animalself, our inner wolf. Mythology and history are filled with stories of utterly bestial, enraged, and unhinged werewolves who simply lost their humanity. *Don't be that werewolf.* Focusing on these powers will help.

Evoking, Invoking, and Shape-shifting

All magick can be seen as coming from within or being called down from outside sources, but the two aspects reflect and synergize each other, as within, so without. The Wildness, Wyrd, and Way must exist within as well as without or our werewolf magick can't succeed. However, when doing ritual work, it is important to note when we are invoking or evoking. Calling up our Animalself and calling down into ourselves the power of the Wolf Spirit are, in essence, one thing but in ritual work are done and felt differently.

We know that the two actions reflect the same truth, but they require different ways to focus our will when being implemented. Think of it like kayaking, which uses a paddle-bar with identical blades at either end. It is really one paddle, but we alternate dipping the left or right blade in the water. These blades can be seen as invoking and evoking.

Different practices, rituals, and spells call for evoking, invoking, or often both, but in a way that is akin to the paddle of a kayak—use them one at a time to keep moving forward. However, werewolf magick is, of course, intuitive. There are no hard or fast rules and so we should always follow our instincts. This reminds us that structure is good, but flexibility is better.

Evoke or Call Up Powers from Within

This is the path of atavistic resurgence, the opening up of the primordial animal powers within our unconscious mind. This is about calling up our animal archetypes and accessing genetic keys to our inner wolf under the guidance of our Animalself. In short, we are calling up from within the deep primal powers by evoking our Animalself with the aid of our will, a manifestation of our higher self. We will be using a variety of techniques, spells, and rites that call for evoking such powers with a variety of strategies. Once we enter the feral realm of evocation, it is important that our Instinct, Intuition, and Insight, guided by our Animalself, help us when things get wild. This is important, because once things start erupting from within us, there are no other guides that really matter because everyone's Animalself is unique.

Evoking includes calling up or inflaming energetic wolf-power into the body from the fire center in the solar plexus. It also involves accessing and calling forth the deep unconscious mind, the group unconscious mind, as well as embedded animalistic genetic information to evoke astral, mental, emotional, and perceived or real physical changes.

Evoking the Double is a slightly different practice than evoking the Animalself or inner wolf-power. The Double is a different animal in that we can call it forth but then invoke it as a separate being outside of our body. In werewolf magick it can also be shaped and empowered as a separate entity to be invoked and ridden. In this case, we call it a Fetch and the process will be described later in the book in chapter 5 on shape-shifting.

Invoking or Calling Down Divine Powers

Invoking Wildness powers is calling into your self external nature powers, often in the form of gods or spirits like the wolf-power, to cause, aid, or facilitate magick to and through you. Rather than the internal eruption of evocation, invocation calls on external natural energies to manifest primal powers with the support and agency of the Animalself. Calling on your personal gods and spirits of nature together to support and empower you in this is a time honored tradition in many Pagan cultures.

Deities such as Faunus, Soranus, or Hekate have been invoked for divinely aided transformation in the past through offerings, prayers, and rituals. This sort of divinely invoked werewolf magick help is woven into several of the rites and spells in this book. Such divine invocations are used to aid shape-shifting but usually in conjunction with evocation as well.

Another use of invoking in werewolf magick has to do with the Double. This is where it can get a little confusing; there are two ways the Double has been traditionally invoked and then used. As mentioned, the Double has always been important in shape-shifting. You can evoke your Animalself as a conscious astral form to do astral work or the werewolf Double can be evoked as a separate wolf form entity and ridden or "worn."

In short, you can evoke your werewolf Animalself as a Double or it can be evoked as a separate wolf spirit and your consciousness can ride it. Think of those witches riding wolves to the astral sabbats. In this way it can be evoked as a separate entity, detached from our body, and ridden or used for various tasks as a Fetch.

The Double, once evoked, can then be treated as a separate entity and be invoked. This is a bit confusing but in line with ancient practices. In traditional magick, one's higher self (the Jungian self) can be evoked and then spoken with as a separate entity and invoked often. Think of it as externalizing a part of yourself and then talking to this part of yourself. We talk to ourselves all the time; this is just a spiritual process of the same sort of thing. Working with the Double in this way, like most werewolf magick, involves invoking and evoking. Here is how:

- The Double is brought forth or evoked through your will with the power of your innate Animalself, empowered and externalized.
- It is then worked with and shaped as a separate spiritual entity or spirit, in our case in a werewolf form.

- When the Double has become strong enough to function independently it is ready to become a "vehicle" for astral work. This can include "remote viewing," far-seeing magick, or lucid dreaming work.

Having discussed the theories and principles of werewolf magick, we are now ready to move forward into the practical aspects of shape-shifting, rituals, and spells. Now we can see what the processes are, the rationales, and what werewolf magick is as a modern, pragmatic system of animalistic shape-shifting magick. To prepare for hands-on ritual work, we will next move on to the practical aspects of werewolf magick, learning about the physical, visual, and linguistic tools needed for the work ahead.

CHAPTER 3

WEREWOLF MAGICK TOOLS

————————— ┼┼┼ —————————

We have been diving into the history, folklore, and principles of werewolf magick, bringing us close to the actual practice. Before we howl and leap into ritual work, let's first see what we will need. What follows are the ritual items, tools, symbols, and unique ways of expression important for the practice of werewolf magick. By finding or, better yet, crafting these items with feral intent and learning about the symbols and nonverbal "language" that infuse werewolf magick, we can enter the realm of the Animalself, which will help us unleash our inner werewolf.

As we walk down this moonlit, tree-covered path of werewolf magick, be aware that your Animalself and the Instinct, Intuition, and Insight that come from it are your best and most potent guides. If you feel that maple leaves or cactus flowers are better for your practice than the oak leaves mentioned in this book, use them instead. Some of these tools and items and ideas come from my own Animalself, the three-eyed wolf spirit within me. Some are influenced by what I learned from historical traditions, like the stang and the use of wolf pelts, but in the end it is up to you and your Animalself. You do not need real wolf bones, for example. Use wool, woven cedar, or some other natural material if you like. The items mentioned here are in sync with werewolf magick and are easy to get but be flexible. If oak doesn't grow near you, then use what is natural to your biome. Nature is the root of our work. Gaia provides everything for werewolf magick, listen to Her with your Animalself, observe Her, be part of Her, like every wolf does. If you do that, you can't go wrong.

At the end of this section you will find the Blessing Ritual for Werewolf Magick Talismans and Tools for empowering any and all of the items mentioned in this chapter. You may use this simple ritual or adapt it or make your own. Mostly I use animalistic nonwords or "werewolf lingo" for such work, as will be described in this chapter. All the items you gather, such as herbs or branches from a tree, need to be honored with a small offering to the plant or tree, the spirit of that place, and to Gaia. Be aware, be grateful. There is no set way to do this magick; let the voice of your Animalself arise! Such blessings or invocations can and should be with howls or silence, not words. Let the voice of your Animalself come through.

The Appropriate Ritual Use of Animal Remains and Their Sacredness

First, let us understand that it is not necessary to ritually use wolf remains. Yes they were used traditionally, but times have changed and wolves are now endangered. Other canines, like coyotes, are not endangered, are prevalent and such remains are easier to get, verify, and just as useful for this work. Remember, you take on the karma of the animal whose remains you use ritually; be careful that it has been appropriately and humanely gathered. All such things should be blessed and charged with the Blessing Ritual at the end of this chapter.

Using Wolf or Other Wild Canid Remains

If you are set on using wolf remains or have somehow gotten some, know this: Since ancient times, using parts of a deceased wolf has been intrinsically linked to werewolf and shape-shifting magick in places where it has been practiced. As werewolf magick practitioners, we accept death, the natural flow of predator and prey, and the eternal cycles of Gaia and of the gods, goddesses, and spirits. We honor human remains of friends and loved ones and the remains of all animal kin the same way. There is a school of thought that we should not use bones, fur, teeth, and other sacred remains of animals in our work, but I find this doesn't make magickal or pragmatic sense in that we are omnivores and most of us eat other creatures and wear leather shoes or belts. Of course, each to his own.

For us, wolves are sacred and cannot under any circumstances be killed for pelts. Long ago, warriors and magic-makers would hunt wolves, but in those days wolves were plentiful, sometimes dangerous, and were treated as honored spirits and kin to be honored and even emulated. Things are far different now as wolves have been vilified, slaughtered, and are endangered.

For this reason it is far more ecologically sound to use the remains of coyotes or other wild canids that are not endangered. The same caveat applies, however: they cannot have been killed simply to sell as curiosities. My coyote skull I use for my practice, for example, was found in the desert.

There is more to be said about treating wolf remains with proper honor, but keep in mind that the same protocols need to be applied to coyote, fox, or other sacred animal remains being used in magick. Such items can easily be substituted in place of wolf remains and should be.

No items from a wolf can be used if there is any connection at all to the murder of that wolf. This is absolutely crucial. It is a moral and spiritual necessity and is also crucial for your magick. If you have any connection with the death of that wolf, a terrible curse may fall upon you. Using items from a long-dead wolf is acceptable, but must be done with clear ritual intent, honor for the spirit of that wolf and awareness of where they came from and how they were obtained. There is no doubt that such items are potent for this work, but the protection of wolves is our paramount concern and is part of honoring the spirits, gods, and traditions we are working with.

If you invoke the Wolf Spirit and suddenly a wolf pelt, bone, skull, or fang comes to you and you have made sure that it is clear of poacher connections, it is important that you do three things out of gratitude and love for its spirit: Take a moment to pray to the spirit of that wolf, make offerings, and give thanks; whenever you work with that item, offer some of the energy of that working toward the preservation of all wolves; contribute to a wolf conservation organization in some way.

The Wolf or Other Wild Canid Belt

The most famous and often mentioned wolf talisman in this book is the magickal wolf belt made from wolfskin. Sometimes it is said to have a buckle, other times it is just tied about the waist. Some refer to symbols or magickal runes inscribed on the backside of the belt. It is often said to be given by the Lord of the Forest to a new werewolf as a talisman for shifting.

Wolf or Other Wild Canid Teeth

These traditional talismans are very powerful and could be worn as part of a necklace, as a pendant for protection or power. Traditionally, wolf teeth are powerful amulets that can also be hung in a home to offer protection and luck. Again, keep in mind that though wolf items are focused on here, coyote, fox, or other appropriately provided or found wild canid remains are suitable and powerful substitutes.

Wolf or Other Wild Canid Bones

If you have a bone it is appropriate to carve or incise it with symbols. Such symbols can come from werewolf magick symbols in this book and/or can be symbols directly given to you by the Wolf Spirit or your Animalself.

A Wolf or Other Wild Canid Skull

A skull contains much more magick, and with that a larger responsibility. A pack—similar to a coven in Witchcraft—may have a skull that is brought out for esbats or sabbats. It is set at the base of a stang—described in the next few paragraphs—facing north. A wolf (or other canine skull) is a very sacred thing and it is crucial that its origins be clear and acceptable. A wolf skull, properly purified and blessed, becomes an image and vehicle for the gods of werewolf magick. If you take up the responsibility for such an item, make sure you can set it up in a shrine and can care for it.

Do you need a wolf skull? No, especially if you cannot guarantee that the wolf or canid was not killed for its remains. I myself use a coyote skull instead of a wolf skull for my shrine for this reason and it is just as powerful in my work and I am guaranteed that it is not endangered. Be flexible in this work as well as realistic.

Ritual Tools and Items

All werewolf magick tools can be charged and empowered with the Blessing Ritual for Werewolf Magick Talismans and Tools at the end of this chapter. In werewolf magick, simply shifting, running about in the forest naked and howling works quite well, but appropriate ritual items help us focus as we ritually invoke our animal powers to arise! These simple items create energetic foci to protect and manifest our magick, and invoke the gods and goddesses we revere and who support our work.

The Altar

Werewolf magick, if not being done outside in nature, is more powerful with a central focus sacred place that accumulates power. A werewolf magick altar or shrine centers the Wildness inside the home and is important for such trance, dream, or Fetch work done inside. My werewolf magick altar, which can be seen on the next page, is about four years old and has grown quickly as the wolfish feral gods gift and guide me. Present are the werewolf god Faunus Lycan and the goddesses Gaia, Artemis, Selene, and Hekate, while the coyote skull centers the energy. The mask is actually used by me for Halloween (Samhain) both ritually and for howling fun with trick-or-treaters. Most of the images and charms here were given to me by fellow werewolf cultists or fans and some were bequeathed to me, such as the wolf fang, fur, bag of runes, and feral charms. In front is a werewolf magick spell candle, which I describe later. As one magickal priestess friend said when seeing it for the first time, "Whoa! Some heavy magick happening here!" Indeed.

The Stang

The stang is a simple forked stick, usually oak, and represents the Lord of the Forest who goes by many names and is sometimes depicted with horns and hooves, as a "green man," or as another feral being. The stang is his symbol and it is his very totem and eldritch center of being. He is of the earth and the representative of animal spirits and primeval forests.

Photo 1: Werewolf Altar

Staves or Wands

Ritual staves or wands are ritually hand cut and whittled stick, often from an oak. They are very powerful tools and important ritual items for werewolf magick. It is recommended that you harvest three ritual staves from a healthy tree at the full moon with offerings to the tree and impromptu invocations of Gaia, the Lord of the Forest, and the Moon Goddess. Each stave should be about the length of your arm from fingertip to elbow, an inch thick, be cleaned of bark, and dyed with natural substances. One is kept plain or dyed white, another black, the third red. These represent the three lunar goddesses of werewolf magick, Artemis, Selene, and Hekate respectively. They can be engraved or marked with symbols of werewolf magick or any that come to you in a trance. If possible, all materials used should be natural. Staves may be used ritually in many ways: as wands, rhythm instruments, stuck into the earth as deity representations, and so on.

It is crucial you find the right tree for the stang. It should be healthy, large, and able to spare a few smaller branches without hurting it. Stop, lean against it, and with your Animalself mentally reach out and touch it and ask for some of its wood. Wait. There will be a sign or signal of acceptance or rejection. Leave an offering, a coin or drop of blood, and many thanks.

The Ritual Dagger

The ritual dagger will be used for cutting tree branches and pricking yourself for blood work, as well as for casting circles, carving ritual items, and for magickal and maybe physical defense. It is roughly analogous to a witch's athame. There are no specific runes or sigils to put on it but of course you may do so as you will. Iron is the best material for the blade since it connects with Ares, but steel or copper blades are fine as well. The handle can be a significant wood like oak, or be of bone, horn, or another suitably natural and animal-centered substance.

A Ritual Journal

As immediate and feral as werewolf magick is, keeping records of omens, chants, experiences, dreams, symbols, images, and the whispers of your Animalself is critical and powerful. Again, find or make a journal that is made of natural materials. Use it often and record everything, including dreams.

Ritual Drinking Cup and Burning Bowl

Most werewolf magick rites and spells call for a ritual cup as well as a plate or bowl to burn herbs in. The primal nature of this magick is such that, again, found items like shells, geodes, or handmade items made from ceramics or wood are best. For example, a real drinking horn would be very appropriate; ornate, fancy chalices, not so much. Rough hewn, natural, simple cups are best. Adding werewolf symbols is fine; let your Animalself help pick them.

Ritual Werewolf Talismans

The best talismans or amulets are created by you and can include any of the werewolf magick symbols mentioned later in this chapter or any other intuitive animalistic symbols you find useful. You can use carved glyphs, a bind-rune, or a wolf emblem of any kind. As with all else, let the inner voice of your awakening Animalself be your guide. Such a talisman could incorporate any werewolf associated stone, such as a moonstone or red jasper. It can be worn in any way, but it is best if it is at least somewhat handmade in a ritual circle and is of natural materials. Silver is also fine to use. The myth that silver harms werewolves was never historically noted and is untrue. Silver is sacred to the Moon Goddess, our loving protector.

Werewolf Herbs, Flowers, Scents, Foods, and Drinks

In this book I note items to be used for werewolf magick exercises, spells, and rituals. They come from a wide variety of sources, some older and traditional, but often I have depended on my Animalself to guide me to what I should use. Do the same. If something feels "right" for your werewolf work, use it. If not, don't. That is how wers roll. Again, listen to the earth in your biome, follow Gaia's guidance. What do wild animals near you use or connect with? Listen to your inner wolf. Some herbs, like rosemary, have traditional magickal associations; others, like mountain ash, appear in old folkloric werewolf spells. As in all things, use what works for you and what nature offers. Experiment with different herbs, much will depend on what is around you. I live in a very lush, wet area but if you live in a desert you will, of course, want to use different items. Consult your local nature and wildlife, and your Animalself.

Werewolfish Flowers, Herbs, and Natural Oils

- Lily of the Valley
- Marigolds
- Azaleas
- Sunflower
- Lavender
- Rue
- Rosemary
- Bay
- Basil
- Sage
- Cinquefoil
- Thyme

Ritual Substances and Offerings

The rule here is to keep everything natural and bless and honor all items in a ritualistic manner in accord with your Animalself when making or gathering them; avoid artificial items. For example, candles should be made of beeswax, herbs should be pesticide free and if gathered, done so with a quiet prayer or a low howl in thanks to the earth. Oils, stones, flowers, herbs, leaves, and so on should be similarly as natural and as pure as possible. It is a good idea to gather such things at full moons if possible but again be flexible and intuitive.

The Infamous Werewolf Salve or Potion

Often in werewolf accounts a magick salve or lotion made from various plants, oils, and so on was given by the Lord of the Forest to an initiate to aid transformation. Many of the traditional ingredients listed are vile, like baby fat. Many contain extreme psychoactive drugs but the salves mentioned in this book will not contain such substances.

In this book a werewolf lotion or salve is part of some spells. Make one yourself with a natural and appropriate massage oil base and add some natural herbal oils you find powerful or important. The ones I can attest to being helpful in shape-shifting include CBD oils, as well as lavender, oakmoss, and ginger oils. It is good to remember that aromatherapy is a powerful and helpful tool in animalistic magick, scent being one of the first senses to be enhanced as we practice werewolf magick. For me, oakmoss evokes the primal forest, as do pine and cedar oils. Find what works for you and try to create and charge your shifting salve on a full moon.

On the Use of Musk

Many sources refer to musk as the scent for wolf or werewolf magick. Because of the horrific way traditional musk was (and in some places, still is) taken, by killing musk deer and removing their glands, I'm against its use. Today, most all musk is synthetic, making it useless for our purposes. There are plants that offer a similar feral scent that may prove useful in our wolfish work; they include more ecological alternatives such as the musk flower, muskwood, or musk seeds from India. I'd also suggest the use of the musky smelling herb rue, sacred to all sorts of feral gods, like Pan.

Werewolfish Stones

My werewolf magick altar is covered with agates, volcanic stones, smooth white stones from the beach, mica, found crystals, and other stones I picked up at magickal places—including a raw moonstone that captured my fancy at a rock shop. These are the stones and amulets I mostly use. The types of stones you use for your practice is up to you and your Animalself, but here are some that I've found helpful:

- Red Jasper
- Onyx
- Crystal, especially if you found it yourself

- Obsidian

- Moonstone

- Found "hole-y" stones (with a natural hole in it)

- Granite

Diamonds are often cited in various places as being a werewolf stone but are problematic on many levels because of the ethics of their origin and the often bloody politics of diamond wealth. If it is raw or you know it wasn't involved in the violent diamond trade, it may be useful, but otherwise choose another stone.

Werewolfish Trees

- Oak

- Cedar (red is best)

- Mountain Ash (Rowan)

- Fir

- Poplar

- Pine

- Hawthorn

- Willow

- Yew

- Juniper

Werewolfish Liquid Sacraments

- Deep rich red wine

- White wine for lunar focus

- Rum

- Liquors of various kinds—especially herbal ones

- Pure natural water, spring water especially; water is crucial, gathered ritually is best

- Fresh juices

- Goat milk
- Hand gathered teas

Werewolfish Food Sacraments

Food that is gathered as offerings or to share is best if gathered by hand. Wolves in general are omnivores but a majority of their diet comes from meat and fish. They have been known to eat most anything but they never eat other wolves, even if they kill them in territorial disputes.

- Raw, dried, or cooked, humanely killed meats and fish
- Eggs
- Fresh vegetables and fruits
- Wild herbs and nuts
- Berries, fruits, and seeds

Werewolf Magick Symbols

Symbols and glyphs are as powerful in werewolf magick today as they were when they were drawn on ancient cave walls. This is because they are not intellectual, logical, or "left brain" activating. Instead, images and symbols appeal to our more fluid and creative "right brain" and are visceral in their power. A symbol is an image that may have multiple meanings, but I use the term glyph to mean symbols that also may have a communicative aspect, like runes. Magick of all kinds is full of symbols, glyphs, and diagrams that fascinate and trigger deep responses. What follows is my collection of werewolf magick images, glyphs, and runes I use in shape-shifting and werewolf work. I've added a couple that appeared in my own visions, but all are mere suggestions. Once called, your Animalself will show you other symbols and guide you in this regard.

Werewolf Symbols and Glyphs

All such symbols can be painted, engraved, carved, tattooed, sewn, or incorporated in other artistic ways for werewolf magick work. They can be added to magickal tools, items, ceremonial clothing—really anything. All such things can be charged with the blessing ritual at the end of this chapter. Here are symbols and glyphs I use with short explanations about the meaning and use of each:

Figure 1: The Triskele

Triskele

The Triskele has three meanings. It represents the three aspects of the moon—new, full, dark—and the corresponsing goddesses invoked. It also represents the three modalities—Wildness, the Wyrd, and the Way—and the three powers—Instinct, Intuition, and Insight.

Figure 2: The Wolf Paw

Wolf Paw

The Wolf Paw represents primordial power of the werewolves, the Wildness, protection, primordial sexuality, power, and shape-shifters.

Figure 3: Werewolf Fangs

Werewolf Fangs

This symbol is used for banishing, protecting, warding, or cursing entities and people who disrespect, seek to harm, or attack any wers or pack. This symbol actively averts/returns any bigotry, hate, or aggression.

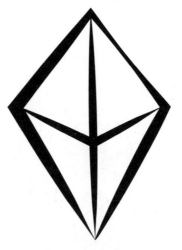

Figure 4: The Eye of the Wolf

Eye of the Wolf

This is a powerful runic symbol of werewolf magick. It represents power, Wolf Spirit, protection, awareness, and the open "third eye" or spiritual focus of the Wolf Spirit. An appropriate talisman or glyph to focus werewolf magick.

Figure 5: The Claw Slash

Claw Slash

This is a symbol used for warding, averting, and marking territory. It signals thoughts like "beware," "back off," "no hate accepted," "our territory," or "piss off!"

Figure 6: The Pentagram (in paw)

Pentagram

This popular occult symbol is an ancient sign that dates back to the ancient Greeks and was associated with Witchcraft in the Middle Ages when it was deeply entwined with lycanthropy. The pentagram is also called "the witches' foot." In werewolf magick it specifically represents the three aspects of the Moon Goddess, the Lord of the Forest, and Gaia, as well as the traditional five elements—air, earth, water, fire, and spirit. Occult folklore has various stories about those who are werewolves being identified by a pentagram on the chest or hands, thus it has become a symbol of werewolfism.[44] In werewolf magick we also see it as the open hand, fingers splayed, meaning "I am a werewolf, both wolf and human and balanced and integrated as one whole." I have depicted it here on a palm, but any pentagram depiction is fine.

Figure 7: The Lit Stang

The Lit Stang

The stang is an exceptionally ancient symbol of the Lord of the Forest, horned/wolf feral god, guardian, and manifester of Wildness, weaver of the Wyrd and breath of the Way. The stang, with a small flame between the horns, indicates the blessing of the Lord of the Forest and that he is awake and aware. This image is often reflected in cross-cultural depictions as the Horned God where a torch, flame, or star is shown between the joyous Lord's horns. I feel it shows the uniting of the Animalself (stang) with the "higher" self (the flame) in balance and harmony.

---

44. Steiger, *The Werewolf Book*, 85.

Figure 8: The Triple Moon

Triple Moon

The werewolf magick triple moon is different in that all three Moon Goddess aspects are entwined with the all-important full moon. It is the full moon that does the best job at parting the veil for shape-shifting and werewolf visionary work, but the moon in all its phases is holy in werewolf magick. It is powerful for visionary, erotic, dream-centered magick, and useful for a variety of spells and protective magicks.

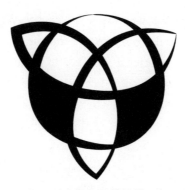

Figure 9: The Wolf Triquetra

Wolf Triquetra

The triquetra symbol is one of the oldest ancient Celtic symbols, dating back to as early as 500 BCE and often depicted in Celtic artwork and textiles. In this particular form the triquetra signifies the face of the Wolf Spirit embodying Instinct,

Intuition, and Insight unified by the pure awareness of the animal-mind manifesting the Way of being without thinking.[45]

Runes, Glyphs, and Other Symbolic Systems In Werewolf Magick

Many symbols and glyphs held a powerful place in ancient werewolf cults just as they do now in modern werewolf magick. Some images, glyphs, or letters that also were used as powerful symbols, such as ancient Greek letters or Norse runes, were used by werewolf cults in their magickal rites and so are appropriate to use if they resonate with your Animalself.

Some of you will be drawn to runes, others to Greek letters, still others to Celtic systems like ogham; it is up to you and your Animalself. It may also depend on the systems you are already using. There are countless other glyph systems, or better yet, you could create your own as your Animalself guides you.

Werewolf Lingo

Your body is the most important tool in werewolf magick and that includes your voice and the gestures you make. Many systems of magick and occult practices focus heavily on invocations and chants in human languages but werewolf magick is a bit different. Some of our rites and spells utilize human words in places; however, the most potent and primal way of truly expressing your Animalself is with animal sounds and gestures. Human language is largely learned culturally, while animal communication systems of barks, whistles, growls, and so on emerge in animals through instinct.[46]

Reconnecting with the long-neglected internal power of instinct is one of the core pillars of werewolf magick. A powerful way to do this is by using what is called "nonverbals" such as gestures and animalistic sounds. In werewolf magick, we mostly use emotionally charged howls, growls, and barks rather than words. We call this werewolf lingo. Escaping the intellectual tyranny of the ego and the higher cortex is key to the atavistic resurgence of the Animalself and thus crucial to werewolf magick. Using uttered nonverbals such as howling and physical nonverbals such as leaping conjures primal feel-

---

45. Ancient-Symbols.com, "Triquetra Symbol."
46. Hedeager, "Is Language Unique to the Human Species?"

ings directly from our deep mind and our Animalself, and does so much more directly than words. Using werewolf lingo also reminds us consciously and unconsciously that we *are* animals and as such, when we are shape-shifting into werewolf trances, we are in the nonintellectual *present*, as are all other animals. Such a powerful yet simple technique stops us from thinking about the past, future, or what we want for dinner, and makes us focus on the here-and-now reality of our existence. Embracing such a wholly present animal consciousness is necessary for werewolf magick.

Growls, howls, and barks, instead of words, also accesses the unconscious mind and deep, genetic-connected atavistic pre-language, pre-civilized centers of the brain or lower cortex, as described by astronomer and author Carl Sagan:

> Deep inside the skull of every one of us there is something like a brain of a crocodile. Surrounding the R-complex is the limbic system or mammalian brain, which evolved tens of millions of years ago in ancestors who were mammal but not yet primates. It is a major source of our moods and emotions, of our concern and care for the young. And finally, on the outside, living in uneasy truce with the more primitive brains beneath, is the cerebral cortex; civilization is a product of the cerebral cortex. which evolved millions of years ago in our primate ancestors. The cerebral cortex, where matter is transformed into consciousness, is the point of embarkation for all our cosmic voyages.[47]

The power and primal intensity of our Animalself can be unlocked by triggering ancient but still extant animalistic parts of your brain. This is a crucial key to shape-shifting because it bypasses the cognitive language centers of the brain and goes right to primordial power, the always-present aspects of the animals we evolved from. The key to werewolf magick is waking those forces up and calling this power forth as our own unique Animalself. This is the purpose, use, and importance of werewolf lingo. To be a werewolf, one must speak, behave, and assume the aspects of a werewolf.

---

47. Sagan, *Cosmos*, 291.

Types of Werewolf Lingo

The following sounds are some of the most useful and common nonverbal communicative tools of werewolf lingo that are referenced in many spells and rituals. Be aware that learning to vocalize unusual sounds takes time and will stretch your vocal cords. It is a good idea to look online for videos of real wolves vocalizing to get in the groove of this work.

Growls and Their Meanings

Everyone knows how to imitate a growl, but can you growl like a wolf or bear? Relax yourself, open your diaphragm, open up your chest, open your mouth, and growl. Place your hand on your chest, loosen your jaw and mouth, and pull your shoulders back. Growl deeper. Relax, but go deeper. Keep trying, don't push or force it. Use deeper breaths, slow it down. Growl, lower, lower, deeper… quieter, then get louder. Drink some warm tea as you work and practice often. Here are some types of growls and what their meanings are in werewolf magick:

- *Calming growl:* Evokes thinking or feeling; also acts like a meditation or wer mantra. To practice it, try doing a low growl, something you'd hear a content dog do.

- *Rumble growl:* This low, deep, almost inaudible growl nearly sounds like a purr. It signifies contentment, contemplation, focus, and simply "being in your skin" when shape-shifting. Practice doing the lowest growl you can as deep in your chest as possible; it should have lots of bass but also be quiet.

- *Agitated low growl:* Use this when you're feeling irritable or need some space. This type of growl can be done with short bursts of low, deep growling with a bit of irritation.

- *High growl:* This growl is used for clear communication, active magick ritual work, and to make a statement. It may signify "We are one!" or "We activate this spell now!" or even "Yeah!" This growl takes place higher in you chest, more excited and upbeat, higher tone. Practice until it feels right for you. Every wolf sounds different.

Note: While these growls serve as a guide, all of these sounds will depend on your own body, vocal cords, and pitch of your voice.

As you practice these growls, also practice growling words. We all growl at people when we are irritated, so begin there. Once you have your growls down, practice saying short phrases like "werewolf magick" lower and lower in your throat as a growl. Can you deepen that phrase into your chest? Keep trying to get the phrase lower, rougher, more animalistic. When it gives you a few shivers, you are there!

All invocations with words used in werewolf magick work should be growled. Developing your "werewolf voice" is quite powerful when saying anything intense. Practice saying normal things like "No!" or "Go away!" in a deep growl with friends and family to see their reactions. When it begins to trigger them emotionally, you have it! Words are power. Growled werewolf words are very powerful.

Howls

Beyond a doubt the most iconic werewolf sound is the howl. There are many kinds of howls. Many of us have howled at rock concerts or ball games, but here is some advice on how to howl; it is an important part of werewolf magick so take the time to practice:

- Stand in a relaxed manner, get loose, and shake yourself if that helps. Pull your shoulders back, tilt your head back, open your arms to open your chest.

- Then, take a really deep breath, inhaling slowly and consistently until your lungs are as full as possible. You need a large amount of air to imitate the volume and duration of an actual wolf howl.

- Cup your hands around your mouth as if you are going to shout and begin howling slowly. Start with a low, mournful note, and then quickly increase your pitch as you go in one long sound until you get that classic awooooooooooo!

- Increase the volume of the howl so that it grows louder and louder. Hold the howl for a few seconds. As you run out of breath, lower your pitch and let the howl fade.

- The longer the howl, the more power and emotion is communicated. There is no one right way to howl; every wolf has a unique howl with slight variations in pitch so other wolves can identify each other.

- Make sure to drink a lot of water to keep your voice clear and your throat cool.

- Don't overdo it at first; you can easily stress your vocal cords.

- Practice a lot and as you do your voice box, chest, and throat will all expand and adjust. You will soon find your howls become deeper.

- Practice doing howls with several notes or pitches, like a short wolf song. This is how packs communicate and express a variety of feelings. Watch videos to see the amazing variety possible.

There are many kinds of howls; you can practice all of them.

- *Howl of joy:* This howl is used when words fail when we are filled with wild exhilaration. This full-body, no-mind, all-out howl will do as the werewolf "Hurray!"

- *Howl of distress:* This howl is used to communicate pain, loss, sadness, depression, and loneliness with slow, mournful, or upset howls.

- *Situational howls in ritual work*: When we are doing werewolf magick rituals, the howl can have nuanced uses and meanings including invoking, praising, banishing, or centering the group or the magick. Some howls may also just be for fun. Sometimes only a howl will express the wild joy of the Animalself and if practicing in a wolf pack, such howls are infectious.

Those are the commonly used nonverbal expressions used in werewolf magick and the most cited in rituals, but there are a few more.

Other Types of Werewolf Lingo

It is possible once you have dived more deeply into werewolf magick you will find yourself uttering primordial sounds you can't imagine now. Watching wolves in their natural state on videos will show you how varied the kinds of sounds they make can be. Here is some other useful and somewhat common werewolf lingo used in werwolf magick:

- *Yip or bark:* Short, staccato, cut-off barks, these sounds often express joy, amusement, playfulness or humor are used for getting attention. Yips or barks can also be used as warnings.

- *Whines:* These deep, guttural whining sounds communicate needs like food, thirst, sleep, or attention. Whines can also be used to communicate empathy.

- *Chuffing:* This sound, a kind of guttural cough, is like canine laughing or gentle mocking. It can represent a kind of eye-roll signifying "Whatever!" or "Oy!"

Werewolf Lingo Intonation and Shifts

Intonations matter when we are speaking in human language. When we say, "I'm great!" with an upward intonation, it shows we really do feel great. When we say, "I'm great," with a sigh and a down monotone intonation, it really means that we are not great at all. Intonation flavors our language and shifts meaning, sometimes a lot. The same is true with werewolf lingo, especially in terms of magick. Adding an ascending or descending intonation shifts the meaning and the magick. Basic patterns of intonation are prefixed with **up-**___ (ascending) or **down-**___ (descending). If a howl listed in a spell or ritual doesn't have a prefix, it is either intoned flat or left up to us to express how we feel.

An ascending inflection often indicates power being raised or offered to a deity. A descending inflection often indicates power being grounded or shared. Some examples of these intonations include the up- and down-growl. The up-growl begins low, rises up, and might be used to banish or push energy out.

The down-growl begins high and descends down and can be used to ground power or end a spell or ritual.

Some rituals or spells call for alternating up/down inflections. The up/down rhythm, much like chanting or singing, communicates and activates the magick in unique ways and is worth experimenting with.

The Growl/Sway Exercise

This is your first werewolf magick exercise; relax and enjoy! You will get your first taste of awakening and evoking your Animalself and you will experience firsthand several of the topics we have been discussing so far. This exercise can be used often in the work to come and can be done any time you want to enter a light werewolf trance.

Setup

This can be done anywhere at any time, but it is best done in a natural place since you are drawing upon the forces of nature. I find practicing this exercise near a tree to be the best. You may want to be alone since you'll be growling and swaying, which may be misinterpreted by bystanders. Try to practice this exercise barefoot if possible.

Items Needed

Relaxed clothing

The Exercise

Stand and breathe deeply. Relax, slouch a bit, bend knees slightly, release all tension. Feel the earth below you, reach down into Gaia and let stress flow from you. Close your eyes. Breathe deeply and in your imagination, visualize your inner animal, your most primal being, as an awakening amorphous beast. Remember when you were completely in your physical body, when you were swimming, hiking or running, making love, dancing wildly, all the times your body, your most animalistic self took over and all intellect was forgotten.

See yourself as this primal being, visualize it as an awakening wolf if you like, and will it to arise and fill you, to take over! Silently call to it and feel it flow up into your mind and body as a warm, sexual, joyful feeling until your thinking fades and you are focused on feelings, sensations, the joyful physicality of your amazing body.

As you deepen and expand your breath, intensely use all of that warm animalistic power to rise up as your Animalself, the animal you are awakening and becoming now. With each inhalation, feel it filling your body and taking over your consciousness. Become wholly your physical self, your Animalself, a different being. Let your ego, conscious mind, and all your mundane human thoughts and worries fade away.

When you feel that you have become your Animalself, barely open your eyes and begin to gently sway back and forth by shifting your weight from foot to foot, knees bent, relaxed. Breathe in time with this swaying as your Animalself takes over. You are like waves in an ocean, rolling back and forth. With each sway left to right, do a low growl with no intonation.

Repeat this sway and growl. Feel yourself relaxing, you are an animal. Feel the rhythm lull you into calm, into a light trance state as you become more feral and less human. Slowly add intonation to your growls. When you shift to your left, do an up-growl; when you shift to your right, do a down-growl.

Now switch if you like; up-growl when you move right, down-growl when you move left. Note the difference in energy and power. Which works better for you? How would you use both ways?

It will take a bit to get used to it, but soon you will be swaying back and forth, up-growling and down-growling. When you feel like you've rocked enough, slow your rocking and let your growl fade to silence, then stop.

Take time to just be an animal while your mind is silent. Feel the breeze and sunlight on your skin, smell the nature around you. Focus on your senses and how truly awake your body is. Enjoy a break from being a human.

When you feel it's time to come out of this light werewolf magick trance and return to normal human consciousness, begin to rock slightly side to side, forward and back. While doing so, stomp on the ground with a foot in a steady and slow rhythm. Do a low rumble-growl with no change in intonation.

As you do so, feel your Animalself sink down into your inner being as your human consciousness slowly rises to the fore. With each stomp feel the trance state fade into the earth. Let your growling fade into deep breathing. When you are "back" as a human, slow and then stop the rocking and stomping and shake your whole body. Feel the earth under your feet and how grounded you are, how quiet your mind is, and how relaxed you are.

This is a simple, but effective, exercise to relax, move energy through you, and most importantly, awaken and call up your Animalself. Try it when you are stressed or feeling down; it will help. Try adding visualizations of yourself shifting into a werewolf while doing this and you will soon feel very werewolf-ish indeed!

Other werewolf magick rituals and spells will build on this simple exercise, but for now experiment with it as often as you like. Play with all the werewolf lingo sounds and be creative; your Animalself will guide you with Instinct, Intuition, and Insight.

Some Interesting Occult Aspects of Werewolf Lingo

Though we are trying to avoid overintellectualizing, this is a book on magick so let's take a higher-cortex moment and think about werewolf lingo in terms of other common magickal or occult systems. In this way, we can add werewolf lingo to our spellcraft or ritual work in most other traditions. Ending a circlecasting with a howl is joyful and powerful!

A howl corresponds with the spirit and is linked to invoking and evoking. It also corresponds with raw power, unity, alarm, joy, and absolute affirmation: YES!

A yip corresponds to the element of air and means happiness, playfulness, agreement, exclamation, or encouragement.

Growling corresponds to the element of earth. It communicates physical action, earthing, empowering, projecting, power, and warnings. It can also communicate anger or be used in moments where you're thinking WTF!

Barks correspond to the element of fire and express happiness, gaining attention, exclamation, playing, and agreement.

A whine ties in with the element of water. It can communicate sadness, need, pain, disagreements, or sympathy.

Blessing Ritual for
Werewolf Magick Talismans and Tools

We end this chapter with our first full ritual. At this point we know where werewolf magick came from, what it is, and the philosophy, ethos, and ideas behind it. We also have delved into the tools, talismans, images, and werewolf lingo that are part of werewolf magick. This is a simple ritual bringing all of this together, a magickal way for you to bless and empower your werewolf tools, talismans, or other items. It is a simple, fun, relaxed first step into real shape-shifting and werewolf magick.

This ritual can easily be used for any werewolf magick talismans, tools, or items that need purification and charging. Of course any animal remains involved should be clean and safe to handle. Note that there are two versions of the rite depending on whether you are blessing animal remains or other items.

Setup

Find a quiet wooded or natural place where you won't be disturbed. A cross-path would be ideal, but not necessary. A backyard, patio, or room with plants would work as well. Make sure you are clean with relaxed clothing.

Items Needed

The tools or items to be blessed

A flat stone, stump, or green cloth made of natural fabric to act as an altar

A small amount of natural salt

A shell or natural bowl to burn dried herbs in

Bay leaves

A tuft of your hair

Optional: A form of divination (runes, tarot, or *I Ching* are recommended, but any will do)

The Ritual

Do this ritual at twilight on or near a full moon. Take your items to the woods or natural spot you've chosen As you enter the natural place to do the ritual, begin to call up your Animalself and it will arise making you aware of your

Instinct and Intuition, and so will provide Insight as you proceed. Set up an altar with your items to be blessed. Lay them out on a rock of some sort. Place the bay leaves in the bowl or shell to the right of the items and the divination tool (if you are using one) and salt to the left.

Sit in silence and breathe deep, let the power of nature feel you, continue to evoke your Animalself, see and feel it stir like a wolf waking up within you. Bring it to consciousness to fill you. Bare your teeth and quietly do a low growl as it fills you.

Sprinkle a pinch of the salt upon the items being blessed and sprinkle some in a circle clockwise around you. Bare your teeth further and intensely up-growl three times firmly to scare away anything negative. Visualize all such unwanted energies fleeing.

At this point, start to do the Growl/Sway Exercise we just learned. Stand, slouch, relax, barely open your eyes, and begin to sway back and forth by shifting your weight, knees bent, legs relaxed. Imagine yourself swaying like a tree in the wind, back and forth, back and forth, and with each move from left to right, quietly low growl without changing the intonation.

When you feel ready, slowly add intonation to your growl. When you shift to your left, up-growl; when you shift to your right, down-growl. Do this until you are in a light and relaxed trance state, consciousness and ego stilled, your mind free of thoughts and stress, your lungs and body filled with the energy of nature and of your Animalself. You are now feeling the beginnings of the first stage of shape-shifting. Do this for as long as you are comfortable, maybe five to ten minutes.

When it feels right, slow the rocking, let the growling fade to silence and then stop. Breathe deeply. Feel your Animalself, the earth under your feet, how grounded you are, and the natural and primal power flowing through you. You will use it now.

Pause for a second and let your Animalself sniff about. Shake the salt off your items into the four quarters and stand on some of the salt. Concentrate on the empowering energy within you and about you; see it flow into the items.

Pause, then exhale with a long low growl. Now you have two options on how to the bless the items depending on whether the items are made of animal remains or not.

If you are blessing an item made of animal remains, use the following directions: Sit with the item and whine as you honor and visualize the spirit of the deceased wolf or other animal. With several low whines, mourn its passing, then with low, down-growls and yips, call its sacred essence to you and mentally offer energy, love, and will in the use of these parts that are no longer needed by the beast.

Do a low up-howl as you ask permission to use the item in the sacred werewolf magick work you are doing, with deep love and respect for the deep magicks you will be immersed in together. If you feel or experience disturbing or angry rejection, dig a hole, bury the item, and silently pray for peace for that spirit. Light the bay leaves and sit in honor until they are finished burning, then low up-howl and leave.

If you connect with the spirit of that wolf and feel a positive energy or blessing from it, yip and howl your joy and acceptance. Make sure to write down any visions, communications, or draw a symbol or even an image of the wolf itself if it reveals such things. This is a potent situation and the item's spirit may honor you with help and ongoing support.

Salt the item again. Hold it in both hands and evoke your Animalself with three long, slow up-howls evoking the Wildness in your loins, rising to the Wyrd in your heart, and flowing from your third eye (the power center or chakra in the center of your forehead) as you call upon the Way. Activate these energies by calling them forth from your body by focusing on the head, heart, and sex—the three body chakras or energy centers—until you are filled with the wolf-power from the item. Close your eyes; focus all the energy as intense, powerful red light into the item. Do a down-howl three times to lock the power in the item.

If you are blessing any items that do not use animal remains, follow these directions: Light the bay leaves in the bowl or shell and do a very low up-howl three times, in this way calling on and thanking the Lord of the Forest, the

Moon Goddess, and Gaia. Visualize their powers responding to the call of your Animalself.

Place a snip of your hair on the burning herb and gently, carefully cense the item to be blessed in the smoke with three passes, quietly low down-growling as you do. Channel your blessing and power flowing directly from your Animalself into the item. During this, entwine your aura into and through the item by visualizing your energy as a strong brilliant light that extends your Animalself energy into the item. It may be visualized as white or another color depending on the item or purpose. Then, feel and see the awakening wolf energy fill the item and glow.

When you have finished this process, rub your face or chest with your hand and then rub the scent and your skin oil into the item while doing a low howl with love and joy as this new sacred item is marked and embraced as part of you.

Hold the item at your heart and lie upon or touch the earth with one hand.

Close your eyes, gently do a low up-growl, and become one with your Animalself as you feel Gaia energy flow up from the earth and embrace you and your new sacred item. Stay in this position a while.

When it feels right, stare at the item you are blessing and close your eyes. If you see a positive image or get a positive feeling, all is well. If the Insight is clear, follow it. However, if the vision, feeling, or insight is troubling, silently ask what is needed to make things right. You may be called upon to do something else with item. Your animal instinct will guide you. It is possible that it is correctly blessed but meant for another person.

When your Animalself lets you know it is time to go, place some of the ashes from the burned herb on your brow, heart, and sex chakras and rub some on the item being blessed to seal it. Then, with low up-growls, offer some ashes to the four quarters of your area to honor Gaia. Then offer some above you to honor the Lord of the Forest and some to the ground beneath you with a low down-growl to give final thanks to Gaia and finally ground all the energy.

Gather up your ritual items, center yourself, and breathe deep a few times. Slowly sway back and forth, letting go of your Animalself and the trance. Slowly touch the earth with both hands, down-growl three times, and as you do so see your Animalself sink into your inner being and curl up in the cave of your deep mind. It is resting but still aware. The trance now fully leaves you. Breathe. As you feel the trance leave you, breathe. Then, quietly down-howl to end the work. Clap three times and go forth with your spiritually awakened werewolf item.

From now on, you should treat this item as sacred, to be kept in a special place, maybe in a special werewolf magick altar or shrine you are creating. All items should be tended to as is appropriate. Listen to your Animalself.

Some Final Words

Give yourself a howl! We have learned a lot, including a bunch of werewolf magick history, ideas, philosophy, and principles in a short time. We discovered the truths about werewolf magick, evoking, invoking, and shape-shifting. Now we also have ideas about how it will all come together in practice. We've also had a crash course on werewolf magick tools and images and lingo to use in werewolf magick. The most exciting part is we now leave the learning of theory and principles behind and get started into real werewolf magick work. We are fully ready to become magickal werewolves through rituals, spells, and shape-shifting practices that activate our Instinct, Intuition, and Insight as our werewolf magick becomes increasingly more powerful and transformative. Awooo!

CHAPTER 4

FREEING YOUR INNER WOLF

———————— ┼┼┼ ————————

In the previous chapter we began the process of awakening the Animalself and learning all about what werewolf magick is and what is needed to practice it. The next step to take before moving into shape-shifting is to discover who we are as a werewolf. Each person is a different wolf, and discovering what your inner wolf is and looks like is crucial in forming a connection with the primal, divine spirit of all wolves. Second, you need to embrace your Animalself as the wolf form that reflects who you are. Third, a key aspect of shape-shifting into a werewolf is being able to intensely visualize what *your* werewolf form looks like. Calling the Wolf Spirit to us and getting its blessing will aid us in all aspects of werewolf magick and knowing what kind of wolf we are helps us visualize, personify, bond with, and evoke our Animalself as a wolf. This will prepare us for shape-shifting work and the werewolf magick to come.

Before diving in, do a little research on the kinds of wolves out there. Which one is most like you? To start you off, here are the most common wolves, including prehistoric ones:

- *Dire Wolf (extinct):* The now-extinct dire wolf was a prehistoric giant wolf. Its scientific name is *Canis dirus*, which means "fearsome dog."
- *The Eastern Wolf: Canis lupus lycaon* is a common medium sized, very social and pack-responsible wolf.
- *The Red Wolf: Canus rufus* is found in the southern part of the US. It has a red-colored coat with coloring around the nose. They are very social, but often hunt alone.

- *The Gray Wolf:* The most common wolf species in the world, they are the direct ancestor of dogs. Found in many places around the world,, the gray wolf comes in many forms depending on where it lives. This wolf is adaptable and has stronger jaws and larger teeth than other species. Gray wolves are social.

- *The Indian Wolf:* These wolves are mainly found in India and are smaller than other wolves. They have a reddish or tan coloring and are found to not be as territorial as other wolves. They are quiet and stealthy, mostly eating small animals, and are very maternal.

- *The Ethiopian Wolf:* This wolf is often mistaken for a fox or a jackal because of its small size, long legs, and a muzzle that is long and pointed. They are brownish-red with some white on their bellies. This wolf is mainly found in Ethiopia and is endangered.

- *Arctic Wolf:* These white wolves are able to handle a punishing climate. Territorial and well adapted for the arctic world, they often roam alone while hunting, but still form packs.

- *Mixed Wolves (Coywolf, Wolfdogs):* Wolves, dogs, and coyotes interbreed and produce viable pups. I have encountered coywolves at a nature reserve and my friend had two wolfdogs. From my observations, they are social creatures and adapt to different environments well.[48]

Calling the Wolf Spirit Exercise

The purpose of this exercise is to call to yourself the great Wolf Spirit, the collective power or egregore of all the wolves that have been and still are. Calling and being blessed by this power offers a wolf empowerment that will aid you with werewolf magick. You will begin to relate to your Animalself as a wolf and this is crucial. Read about wolves and werewolf folklore. Do this intensely for several days before trying this exercise to get yourself into the wolf mindset.

---

48. Wolf Worlds, "Types of Wolves."

SETUP

Practice this exercise on a warm day near or on a full moon. Find a natural place, the wilder the better, but a local wooded park would be fine too. If you go into a dense park or woods, you do not need to go alone; others may come with you for safety, but should not observe your ritual since it is for you alone. You will be looking for a place in nature where you can avoid other people for about an hour. If you are going into a remote wilderness, plan your trip carefully. Go when the weather is mild and when you'll have plenty of daylight. Hike as deep into the wilderness as you safely can. Doing this at night is more powerful but it can be done in the daytime for safety reasons.

ITEMS NEEDED

Appropriate hiking equipment

A daypack

A natural altar, like a stump or stone

A small piece of fresh raw meat, well wrapped

Plenty of water

Raw natural foods for you, such as fruit and nuts

Your journal

THE EXERCISE

Hike until you find a place where you can safely leave other humans, maybe ducking off a trail a bit, but not too far. Find the right power spot for your work. Use your intuition. When you have found a place where you can meditate, set up a small natural stone or piece of wood as an altar, facing north if possible.

Sit and meditate on the beauty and power of nature, and of Gaia.

Do some deep breathing, down-gowl with every out breath and let the stresses flow from you into the Earth. Let the growling fade. Feel the energies of nature around you. Let them fill you as you breathe deeply. Place your hands upon the ground and feel Gaia's power fill and connect you with all wild things. Focus on wolves and the intensity of your desire to invoke the Wolf Spirit.

Remove your shoes and feel the earth. Reach to the sky and feel the wild energies fountain up from the earth through you into the heavens. Open up your heart, mind, and body to the joy of Wildness and the Wolf Spirit. Softly up-howl three times as you invoke the Great Wolf Spirit to you. Down-howl once and lay out the small piece of raw meat and a cup of water for the Wolf Spirit on your simple natural altar.

To clear the area of stray energies, up-growl three times and turn about counterclockwise.

Now, do the simple Growl/Sway Exercise from the previous Werewolf Tools chapter. As you continue, enter a light trance to feel and see your Animalself rise within you, maybe in the form of your chosen wolf form.

You will be able to sense and maybe even faintly see the energies about you.

Let the growling and swaying slow then stop and now stand, filled with your Animalself.

Raise your arms and silently, with your Animalself mind, call on the Lord of the Forest, the Moon Goddess, and Gaia to help you call the Wolf Spirit. Pour out a little water onto the altar and softly up-howl and continue slow, soft up-howling as you call to the Wolf Spirit.

Close your eyes; keep howling. After a time it will now come to you. You will know; there will be a clear sign. Maybe it will be a strong gust of wind, the cry of an animal, or a surge of energy in your body. If your hackles rise or you get goosebumps, it is a good sign. When you feel the Wolf Spirit's presence, open your eyes, offer the meat to this ancient spirit with a gesture of open hands and honor it with three low down-howls.

When done, commune with the Wolf Spirit silently, close your eyes, and silently ask for its blessing in your werewolf magick and in shaping your Animalself as a wolf form. Let the Wolf Spirit and your Animalself integrate in complete silence. Sit with it until it leaves you, then quietly up-howl a thanks.

Be still. Breathe. Eat some food and drink water. Feel the Wildness and let the power of the full moon fill you. Take out your journal and write down your experiences, visions, and whatever came to you. Maybe sketch what your Animalself wolf spirit looked like.

When you're ready to go, touch the earth with both hands and silently thank the Lord of the Forest, the Moon Goddess, Gaia, and the Wolf Spirit. Softly down-growl three times and let all the excess energy fade into the earth as your Animalself withdraws.

Do the final rocking part of the Growl/Sway Exercise to return your human-self. Pack everything, check the area to make sure nothing has been left, and leave the meat offering as it is or toss it into the woods.

Have a wonderful hike back and go home and rest. Think about being a werewolf and what comes next on the werewolf path. That night, you will likely dream of the Wolf Spirit or maybe your own Animalself. Whenever you awaken, write down your dreams.

Werewolf Dream Spell to Meet Your Inner Wolf

As you continue down the werewolf magick path you will need to invoke the Wildness, Wyrd, and Way to discover your werewolf self because these are the three manifestations of nature that will help you discover it. This spell will open up the portals of the unconscious through dreams to further the process and evoke your deep mind to summon your sleeping Animalself. It will strengthen your Animalself and strengthen your werewolf power.

Setup

Do this spell in your own bed, or if you're adventurous, do it when camping out overnight. This spell is best done on a full or near-full moon, but any time you feel you need to use it is fine.

Items Needed

Three oak leaves, one you will keep (other leaves can be used as a substitute)

A small beeswax candle

Some oakmoss oil or lavender oil

A journal to write in

The Spell

First, place all the items on a side table next to your bed (or sleeping bag) as you like. At twilight, take the oak leaf you will keep and go for a short walk to where there are some trees. Breathe deeply and let the aura of nature fill you. Meditate on the Wildness inside as your Animalself curled up as a wolf. Do a low up-growl as you walk.

See your inner Animalself wolf stir as you walk in nature and silently call to it to come out and enjoy the trees and fresh air. See it fully awaken and evoke again with a few low up-growls. Think on all the times as a child you were wild and feral, climbing trees and running about. Your nascent Animalself will be drawn to such wild memories and will begin to rise up within you; encourage it. Speak no words.

After your energizing twilight prowl, place an oak leaf on either side of your bed, keeping "your" leaf with you. Up-growl three times intensely as you slowly turn around counterclockwise and see your inner Animalself chasing off any unwanted energies to protect you.

In silence, return to your bed. Sit upon it and put some of the oil on the candle, your forehead, heart, and lower belly. Then light the candle and as you do so, growl these words:

Wolf who lays within me deep
Awake, arise, and fill my sleep
Join with me, you who are wild
I howl to thee, I am your child!

Draw the Eye of Wolf glyph with the oil on your oak leaf and afterward, touch it briefly to the candle flame three times, making sure not to burn it, growling each time:

Animalself wolf-self, come to me
Awake and arise that I may see,
Come to me as I call to thee!

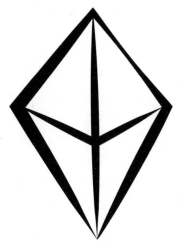

Figure 10: The Eye of the Wolf

Stop and be silent. Wait for an inner sign that you were heard, then sit quietly, and stare at the faint Eye of the Wolf glyph on the leaf and see it come alive, glowing red until it fills your mind. Blow out the candle. Close your eyes, breathe deeply, lie down and hold the symbol image in your mind, still glowing red. See it sink down, down, down into the darkness.

Be still and silent and relax your breath. Place the marked leaf under your pillow. Continue to breathe deeply and rhythmically. Silently call to the Wolf Spirit within you to come to you. Fall asleep with this in your mind.

You may wake up several times during the night. Each time you wake up, write down any dreams or images that come to you in your journal. You will likely get some wild dreams and hopefully meet your inner wolf and run with it or *as* it! It took me several tries, but I eventually was able to run as a werewolf across some fields in a dream! It was a real breakthrough and I awoke with a smile.

The next day, go to a natural place and bury the oak leaves at the foot of a tree, oak if possible, thanking the Lord of the Forest, the Moon Goddess, and Gaia for helping you meet and work with your Animalself. Do this exercise as often as you like to strengthen your bond with your inner wolf.

Becoming Your Wolf

Living organisms store similar genetic information using the same nucleotides that make up DNA and RNA. This is compelling evidence of the shared ancestry of all living things. Evolution of higher life-forms requires the development of new genes to support different body plans. However, humans and canines, like other complex organisms, retain many of the same genes because most of them govern core bodily functions important to our physical body, like breathing or digestion, and are carried over from their primitive past.

The upcoming Deep Wolf Scrying Exercise will be a gene-centered psychic process that will aid in shape-shifting rituals. The ideas behind this we learned at the beginning of the earlier werewolf lingo section, in the Werewolf Magick Tools chapter.

In magick the rule is "as within, so without," meaning that the work you do in the perceived external or outer world will be experienced or even replicated within yourself and internal magickal work manifests in your outer reality. This exercise is all about interior discovery and transformation that will, in shape-shifting and other werewolf magick, manifest in your outer reality.

While the outer werewolf magick experiences are powerful and may in fact give enough concrete results for the reader, this inner alchemy offers you a way to access the deep primal layers of the animal genes within us. This will help you balance and integrate your Animalself that is embodied in your very genes, This in turn informs and enhances your werewolfery in the outer world, like when you're prowling in the woods.

Within the structure of our physical biology lurks the DNA of every animal that went into making us who we are through evolution. This is a powerful physical and therefore magickal link. Epigenetics—the study of how genes can change an organism—states that our DNA is not a static frozen template; it can and does change as we live through interactions with our environment and from external energies. Through magick you have more control over and access to your genetic information than you realize.

Our human brain is a result of eons of evolution and this is especially germane to the "primitive brain" (the "reptile mind" described by Carl Sagan) or lower cortex. This is where the Animalself exists and where to access your inner wolf. This is the science behind shape-shifting. In a 2005 study conducted at Massachusetts Institute of Technology looking at learning processes, results showed more interactions between higher cortices and part of our primitive brain. The findings "suggest that new learning isn't simply the smarter bits of our brain such as the cortex 'figuring things out.' Instead, we should think of learning as interaction between our primitive brain structures and our more advanced cortex. In other words, primitive brain structures might be the engine driving even our most advanced high-level, intelligent learning abilities."[49]

The third angle on this deep internal alchemy is the group unconscious mind. Carl Jung believed that just as our human consciousness has evolved over the ages, we built upon the consciousnesses that came before us and are still existing within the group unconscious mind. Thus we still have access to the most primitive parts of our unconsciousness. As Jung writes:

Just as the human body represents a whole museum of organs, each with a long evolutionary history behind it, so we should expect to find that the mind is organized in a similar way. It can no more be a product without history than is the body in which it exists. By 'history' I do not mean the fact that the mind builds itself up by conscious reference to the past through language and other cultural traditions. I am referring to the biological, prehistoric, and unconscious development of the mind in archaic man, whose psyche was still close to that of the animal.[50]

As we explore the externalized methods and practices of magickal shape-shifting, you can also dive deep and internalize this process by accessing both the DNA program within you and the group unconscious mind, the two being inextricably linked.

By diving into the deepest part of your mind, reaching way past the "human mind" into the deeper strata where the genetic, psychological animal instincts lurk, you can find, commune with, and form a lasting internal bond with your

---

49. Massachusetts Institute of Technology, "Primitive Brain Is 'Smarter' Than We Think, MIT Study Shows."
50. Jung, Man and His Symbols, 67.

Animalself and bring all of that to the fore. We call this shape-shifting. What follows is an exercise that was created for deep-mind genetic exploration and regression.

The Deep Wolf Scrying Exercise

Setup

You'll need to prepare a *very* quiet and *very* dark place where you can be immersed in hot to warm water. A bathtub is fine, but a hot tub works best for longer sessions if one is available. You must make sure that you will not be disturbed for one to two hours. Read this exercise carefully because you will need to remember it. You won't be able to read it during the exercise since you'll be in a tub or water. The more you practice this exercise, the deeper you will go each time.

Items Needed

A small altar set up as you like with the following:

- A wolf image or talisman on the altar
- A small black candle
- A small hand mirror
- A journal to write in later

Sea salt

A sleep-mask or blindfold of some kind

A little dried lavender and something to burn it in

A towel, warm clothes, and a quiet place to relax afterward

A container to mix salty bathwater and lavender ashes at the end

The Exercise

Prepare everything, set up the altar, and then fill the tub with hot water, the hotter the better so that it will stay warm for as long as possible. Take your clothes off, light the candle and herb, turn off the lights, shut the door, and scatter a big handful of salt in the tub. While mixing it in, growl the following invocation:

Out tout
Throughout and about
All good come in,
All evil stay out.

Now, with your hands raised, evoke your Animalself with three low up-howls. Do the Growl/Sway Exercise found in chapter 3 but don't end the light trance by rocking.

Cast a magickal circle with the candle that encompasses the whole room. Call on the great primal Gaia with low howls, yips, and growls erupting from your inner wolf, charging the circle as the body of Gaia and the bath as the womb of Gaia. Then, while still in a light trance, carefully enter the water. Shift to a low rumble growling, like a wolf purring.

Wear the eyeshade so you have utter darkness, still rumble-growling. Relax all your body parts with rhythmic deep breathing. If you know any, follow a relaxation exercise you've done before.

After you've relaxed your entire body, mentally see yourself slip back in evolutionary time. First see yourself as you are, then as a primitive hominid, then as an ape, then as a lesser large mammal. Do this until you have slipped back into an ancient wolf form. Hold that form and note what you are thinking and feeling.

Once you are in your ancient wolf form go deeper and deeper into it. Do so by growling deep in your chest the sound "MA" over and over. Every utterance takes you deeper. Completely become your Animalself. Forget your human form, embrace, enjoy, and experience all the senses and primitive feelings embodied in your wolf-self. Do this until your chattering ego goes quiet.

Be utterly still and vacant. Wait. You will enter the primal consciousness of a wolf; experience that intimately and so gain "wolf wisdom."

Learn.

Become.

Be.

When you are ready, pick up the mirror from the altar and look into it. Stare into the mirror and *see* your new werewolf reflection there. Meditate on the wolf consciousness and wisdom you attained. Explore this new existence in silence with no human words.

When you feel you are ready to end the exercise, visualize yourself evolving from this wolf form to a larger mammal to an ape, a hominid, an early human, and then to yourself. Reenter your human-self, *but with you is your wolf-self too.*

Growl "HA" three times. Integrate the human and wolf; see and feel yourself as one whole being, a werewolf. Sit up and adjust, then slowly and carefully arise from your tub, the waters of the primal sea, the body of Gaia. You are reborn.

Slowly, get out, and dry off. Do a low rumble growling and gently rock back and forth while tapping a foot in rhythm and feel yourself return to full human form and consciousness as your Animalself withdraws. Let everything fade to silence. Take your time. Silently thank Gaia and the Wolf Spirit, and blow out the candle. In silence, write down your experiences in your journal.

When you've finished writing, sprinkle a little of the salty bathwater about counterclockwise and down-growl three times to disperse the energies. Put some of the salty "womb" water into a container with the lavender ashes. Give a silent thanks for now holding one of the keys to the direct wolf wisdom as an awakened part of yourself.

Later on, go outside and find a tree. With love and will utter a long, low up-howl to Gaia and pour out the water from the container at the foot of the tree. Lope forth, a true embodied aware-wolf! Constant meditation and ritual use of what you have received is important. Your journal should be kept and reviewed.

Finding Your Wolf-Self Spell

This is a spell to aid you in finding your true wolf form and visualizing it clearly to aid the process of birthing your werewolf self. Everyone has an inner wolf and if you are reading this then yours is waking up and emerging. This spell is to further bond and manifest your wolf-self so that it can manifest clearly when you become a wer. The images of your wild self that come to you will be personal and will help you visualize and manifest your astral werewolf form as you move further into werewolf magick. The goal, in short, is to keep working on what your inner wolf is like and to discover deeper things about yourself as an evolving werewolf.

Setup

Before you do this spell, research the many kinds of wolves that are out there in nature. Review the kinds of wolves in the world listed at the beginning of this chapter. One of these may enthrall you immediately, come to you in dreams, or just feel right. It is important to access your unconscious mind to see what kind of wolf you really are as opposed to the wolf you wish you were.

Items Needed

Some dry lavender flower-heads or lavender oil

A small mirror

The Spell

It is best to do this in a natural setting like some woods, a hiking trail, a forested park of any kind, or your backyard. However, it can also be done in a room with plants if the window is open. This spell should be practiced someplace where other animals exist. Practice this spell at twilight so that you have just enough light to see. Find a crosspaths if possible with something nearby to sit upon. You must be alone and undisturbed.

Sit quietly, close your eyes, breathe deeply, and open up your senses to nature and all the natural sounds, smells, and sensations around you. Feel the Wildness flow into you from the earth and the trees. Let all stress fade. Breathe deeply, relax, let your Animalself arise.

Take some lavender, crush it, then smell it deeply. Rub a little scent on your third eye or forehead and rub some on the back of the mirror, then sprinkle some in a clockwise circle around you, saying:

Werewolf of crossroads
Set my mind free
Reveal my wolf face
Io Hekate, Io Evoe!

Now, close your eyes, and regress to your Animalself. You are not human but animal. Breathe deeply. Silently evoke your Animalself to rise and fill your mind as a wolf. Breathe deeply as you dive deep. As you do this, something in you may start to stir and an image will arise. Look and see yourself as the wolf you are.

With each deep breath you fall deeper into your wolf-self; with every breath you are less and less human. You are becoming a primal animal, following your nature. Put the small mirror in front of your eyes and slowly open them. You'll see before you a face that is morphing into a werewolf. Watch the shift! Are you a grey wolf? A white arctic wolf? A black timber wolf? Note the color of your fur, notice your expanded senses, look deeply into the eyes which are your eyes; growl hello to your werewolf self! Hold and solidify this image. Put your finger to your lips; you are one.

When the image begins to fade, let it go and begin returning to your human form. Close your eyes; rub a bit of lavender on your third eye and sprinkle it about yourself. Then crush more of it and breathe the scent in several times. With every breath, return to human. The fur is gone; your eyes become human.

When you're finished with the spell, sprinkle the last of the lavender counterclockwise about you, thanking the goddess of wolves, Hekate, and the spirit of your special wolf spirit. Silently ask it to teach and mentor you in becoming become a wer. Touch the earth, let any excess energy sink down, thank Hekate and Gaia, and go forth.

Awakening Your Inner Werewolf Spell

This spell will work on continuing to open your Animalself and the werewolf magick growing within you. Your inner wolf may take time to fully coalesce, emerge, and bond itself with you as you awaken as a true werewolf. For so long humans have suppressed their Animalself, so this bond takes deep work. At this point your inner wolf is a significant power as your shadowy Animalself begins to seriously manifest. The feral part of your yourself will become more pronounced and will indeed emerge through a more natural animalistic physicality and more sensitive primal feelings. Such forces and instincts may change the way you behave, and feel and see the world. This may color your personality a bit and you may start growling and howling a bit more. It is hard to hide the werewolf vibe once you have called it up. Of course, by opening your wolf- power, you will likely become more energized and more emotionally, physically, and spiritually open—all good things—which may pleasantly surprise your friends. It is wonderful to become a more honest and active wolfish person.

Here are a few things you should know before doing the spell because it draws on Norse mythology. The werewolf god in Norse magick is Woton or Odin, the "All Father" who could shape-shift into a wolf, wore wolf skins, and had two pet wolves, Geri and Freki. The word "ulf" used in this spell, meaning "wolf" in Norse, and the Nine Worlds in the Norse religion were all parts of the great tree Yggdrasil. The gods live in Asgard and we live below, in Midguard, two of the Nine Worlds, something you likely know from Thor movies or comics.

This spell also calls for the use of the Algiz rune. Runes are the sacred Norse alphabet imbued with both divinatory and magickal powers after being discovered by Odin as he hung for nine days. The runes were often used individually or combined into "bindrunes" for spells. One of the most common was Algiz, a trident-like rune of immense protection and help.

Setup

For this spell, like many, a wild wooded place or any natural place where you can be alone would work great. There should be a tree nearby and a spot near an intersection of paths would be beneficial. Twilight would be the best time, but do it when it works or feels right to you.

Items Needed

A special stone or crystal. It would be most potent if it is one you found. You
may also use a moonstone, red jasper, or another stone.

A small amount of natural tobacco, no chemicals (tobacco is sacred to Mars
and thus werewolf magick, but you need not smoke it)

A journal

Know the Algiz rune:

Figure 11: The Algiz Rune

THE SPELL

Hold your stone in your hand, breathe deeply, relax, and open your mind. Call
up your inner wolf until you feel it arise and you are filled with the image and
power of your Animalself. Become your wolf-self, feel it happen, see it in your
mind's eye, become it. Take your time. Quietly and rhythmically down-growl
multiple times, like a mantra. You can also do the simple Growl/Sway Exercise
to help you deepen this light trance if no one is nearby.

When you have let your ego take a back seat and are filled with your
inner wolf, open your wolfish eyes and focus on the stone in your hand. Low
up-growl several times and as you do so, fill it with your inner wolf-power and
see it glow. Hold up the stone and trace the Algiz rune in the air before you.
Visualize it as glowing with white, purifying light. As you do so, growl the
word Algiz. See yourself and all around you filled with light, feel the protective
primal power wash over you, banishing all human negativity. Light the tobacco
while reciting the following invocation:

By the Divine Ulf-Self!
Algiz, bring freedom and truth!
By Geri and Freki and the Ulf-Self!
Algiz, freedom and truth!
By the One-Eyed Wolf-Lord of Nine Worlds
Algiz, freedom and truth!
By the Light of The tree

May my wolf roam free
Algiz-Ulf light, so may it be!

Wave some of the smoke about you. With the stone, trace the Algiz rune on your heart and visualize it glowing white upon your inner wolf, feeding it power, freeing it, and making it stronger. Close your eyes and see yourself as a werewolf and raise your arms. You have become the glowing Algiz rune! Absorb the light and rune into your werewolf self. Quietly intone this sacred sound of Algiz: "Aluu!"

Cross your arms over your chest. Breathe deeply and let the light and your werewolf self be absorbed into you. Let the wild wolf energy calm and slowly subside as rationality arises. If you are alone, stand and shake like a canine and let all the unwanted stuff fly off you. Low growl three times and stomp your feet to earth yourself. Thank Gaia silently.

Write down everything you saw and felt in your journal. It will be useful for later werewolf work. To end the spell and banish excess energy, light the tobacco again and wave it about you, saying:

By the Runes and the Wolf God of the Nine Worlds
Algiz, bring the light, banish all fright!

Go forth.

Werewolf Restrictions Release Rite

Part of preparing to work seriously with werewolf magick is letting go of human restrictions that stifle you. To embrace the Animalself you need to break out of your programming and limited human-headspace. This exercise will help remove blockages and open the way for more feral, freeing werewolf energy.

As your Animalself arises and you become more wolfish, it is common to feel things more intensely and be triggered by human restrictions, prejudice, social norms, and the like. Do this exercise when things start to really trigger or depress your Animalself or when you feel trapped—like a wolf—by oppressive environments.

Setup

This can be done at night or at twilight on a waxing or full moon. Do this rite in a wooded or other natural outdoor place where you will be alone, if possible. It's also beneficial for the rite to do it near an intersection of paths.

Items Needed

Some food—raw seeds, nuts, or berries—for local animals

Some red wine (in a container if you are doing this in the woods)

To supercharge this work, put a few drops of your blood or sexual fluid into the wine before you do it.

Your ritual knife

Some pure water

The Rite

Go to the wild or natural place you've chosen with your items. Find something natural to use as an altar to put your things on or use an altar cloth, then center yourself. Start the Growl/Sway Exercise, but don't end it until the end of this rite.

Let your inner wolf arise within you. It will likely be an upset and irritated wolf! Spin around counterclockwise and up-growl intensely, claws bared, banishing anything that would dare interfere with this work!

Then, calmly center your now wer self, breathe deeply, and low grumble growl to focus. Scatter the food in a clockwise circle about you, seeing this food form a loving green circle as well as an offering to the spirits and animals of nature.

Grab your wine and then begin breathing deeply, sway, and unleash your upset inner wolf. In a growl, recite the following:

> Greatest feral Woodland God
> Blessing every step I trod
> Mother Moon feed my trance
> Gaia, fill my dance
> Release all ills, on paws I sway
> Begone restrictions, swept away!

Spill out a little of the wine to each quarter of your area while saying these lines:

To the east:
I exist, in the howl I sing
The breath of winter, the winds of spring
 (up-howl)

To the south:
I exist in the heat of fire
By scarlet eyes and blood-boiling higher
 (up-howl)

To the west:
I now embrace holy moon daughter
Leaping streams and tide pull of water
 (up-howl)

To the north:
I exist with paws and claws in earth
Leaping as a Wolf, primal rebirth
 (up-howl)

Drink some of the wine and pour some of it out as an offering to the Lord of the Forest, the Full Moon Goddess, and Gaia to help free you, up-growling three times. Then growl the following invocation:

By dance and howl and full moon power
By prowl and stalk and fated hour
All anger, all hate, blood madness, ill fate
I release to the sky, I release to the moon!
Giving all to Gaia, by werewolf rune
By claw and fang and dreamtime will
I'm washed in red rain, rage be still
O Faunus Lycan, I howl to thee!
From binding restrictions may I be free!!!

Now, take off your clothes or at least as many items as possible. Then, get wild! Perform a wild howl dance as you will! Let your werewolf self take over! Dance, spin, leap, growl, howl, sweat, and release all that is restricting, binding, angering, oppressing, or inhibiting you! Offer your wild dance to the moon, the forest, and the earth, but don't use any words. Only use howls, growls, barks, flailing furry arms, paws, and flashing fangs. When it feels right, collapse onto your paws and knees and send all leftover energy down to the earth until you are empty of all that bothered and tormented you.

Then, in stillness, pull up from the earth calm, clear, cool centeredness. You are Gaia's child, Her wolf; honor Her silently.

Using the ritual knife, cut off a piece of your hair, release it into the air to the moon and with joy up-howl away all that restricts you. Stand tensed and in full wildness, your fur, fangs, and paws all feeling the fresh breeze. You are now free to be a werewolf! Howl at will. Now, in fully wild wer form, throw your hands up and embrace all of the Wildness about you as well as the full moon above you. Growl the following invocation:

> By howl by blood by moon tides and wood
> By spirits of wildness, both dark and good
> By the fury and power erupting within
> I release all my chains, all restrictions and sin
> As open as nature, I lope as a beast
> I honor all life, the greatest and least
> In my heart the Wild God now grows as a tree
> From traps and cages, I now run free!

From the center, run about in a counterclockwise spiral going farther and farther out and then keep running down a path. Howl, growl, yip: be free! When you feel tired, rest. Be calm and become one with the now-dark forest; let this reddish energy sink into the earth and feel your soul drift toward the full moon like mist. Feel the calm of the beast settle upon you.

Now, slowly return to the circle. Rock, stomp, and breathe as you "watch" yourself losing the fur and claws and fangs as your Animalself withdraws, becoming human again. Take a second to drink some water—you'll need it! Then put on any clothes you abandoned, gather your items, and make sure to leave no trace. As your prepare to leave, do a low down-howl to send your thanks to the wild gods and goddesses who have helped you. Pour out the last of the water and go.

Next Steps

You have now entered the gateway to the "inner sanctum" of werewolf magick and have been moving forward in the process of unleashing and bonding with your inner wolf. This is a key process in truly becoming your werewolf self. You have reached out to your Animalself in the form of a primal wolf, invoked and freed this inner wolf, and bonded with it. This process is something that is not immediate, nor does it happen in one or two sittings. These practices and spells can and should be done a number of times until real, spontaneous success is deeply felt by you and validated by your Animalself. Be aware that you will experience breakthroughs and "aha moments," but repeating these practices until your inner wolf lets you know that you have reached your goal will prepare you to move to the crucial step of shape-shifting.

CHAPTER 5

SHAPE-SHIFTING

———————— |︱| ————————

et's take a minute to regroup and review before we dive into serious, practical shape-shifting magick. You might be surprised to know that we've
already been doing some light shape-shifting as we've worked on calling forth
our Animalself. We've been growling and swaying to bring that inner wolf to
the surface, and in the process, practicing light shape-shfting.

The growling and swaying helped us slide into light werewolf trance states
while letting our deep, wolfish Animalself arise and our troublesome ego move
to the back seat. With that we have already started moving into shape-shifting.
Now, we are prepared to dive seriously into shape-shifting. As you'll see, the
deeper and more feral you get, the more intense and enjoyable shape-shifting
will be. The more you do it, the better you'll get. With these processes, we are
learning to be better animals. Everything we have learned and cultivated up to
this point can now be called upon to help us shape-shift as our inner Animalself
rises to the fore. With all this info and practice under our belt, we are ready for
our complex shape-shifting.

Wolf-Power Exercise

Before we move into shape-shifting rituals, we need to learn about the wolf-
power that helps make serious shape-shifting happen. Many systems of spiritual work recognize the "cauldron" or the center of energetic power that is
in the lower belly or solar plexus. Sometimes also called chi, this energetic fire
flows through our body infusing it with vibrant life. As a main power source of
werewolf shape-shifting, we call it the wolf-power.

Meditate on these thoughts before starting this exercise: Learning to use the wolf-power to power up your shifting is what this practice is all about. Strengthening the spiritual, physical, psychological, and energetic aspect of your werewolf self is an ongoing working of werewolf magick. All of the techniques you have learned and will learn can be supercharged and deepened by generating and directing the bioelectric energy of your wolf-power.

This exercise focuses on fully triggering the fire center or "furnace" of wolf-power. Located just behind your navel in the solar plexus, this center of our energy body (called "dantien" in Chinese) can be focused on and stoked to make the wolf-power flow more intensely through the body, thus giving us the force we need to shape-shift our etheric body according to our will. In this way your primal body can be empowered and changed. Activating this with will and visualization, guided by your unleashed Animalself wolf, will open a flood of wolf-power that then inflames and shapes the energetic and astral body. Doing this while entering a trance, immersing the ego, and unleashing the Animalself can be used to manifest shape-shifting. By utilizing the atavistic power unleashed through the crackling energy of our wolf-power focused with will, visualization, and magick, we can clothe ourselves in any werewolf form we wish. This wolf-power center is considered the seat of will, fittingly, and is a primary "engine" for shape-shifting in werewolf magic.

SETUP

Do this exercise in a quiet, private, and warm place where you can lie in silence and not be disturbed. A bed may be the perfect spot for this.

ITEMS NEEDED

A side table to put the items on

A glass of water with salt in it

Pure water to drink before and after

A small red candle

A clean white hand cloth

A werewolf talisman (or another charged werewolf magick item)

It is best if you wear your werewolf magick talisman to help protect and empower your work. It is a clear signal to your conscious and unconscious mind that you are calling forth the wolf-power for shape-shifting. Do this exercise several times before moving on to other shape-shifting ritual work. The more you do it, the more potent your shape-shifting will be.

THE EXERCISE

Banish, clear, and protect your space by sprinkling salt water around you clockwise with three strong up-growls. Visualize all the energies fleeing and a circle of light around you. Growl the following for setting intention while lighting the candle:

I am Lupercai
I am Lupercai
A Clawed One
A Horned One
A Wild One
A Wolf's-One
A Terrible One!
Wild Wolf-Power
Transform me
As I will
So may it be![51]

Take all your clothes off, lie on your bed, close your eyes, and focus on your body. Meditate on what you now know about the wolf-power and shape-shifting. Breathe deeply. Hold. Exhale deeply. Hold and repeat eleven[52] times, each time relaxing more deeply while sinking into your inner mind.

Eyes closed, totally relaxed, find in your mind's eye the glowing fire that is your energetic gut center at your solar plexus. Now find it with the tips of both hands. Hold them there and feel the smoldering wolf-power. Connect with it.

---

51. *Lupercai* means "werewolf priest" in Latin.
52. In several occult traditions eleven is the number of magick, hence why I suggest using it for this practice.

Continue breathing deeply in and out as before, but this time with each in-breath, see and feel the fiery wolf-power growing larger. With every out-breath see this power sending out glowing rays of light into your legs, loins, trunk, arms, and head.

Feel this expanding wolf-power energy flowing out from your energy-center and spreading through your whole body as gentle waves of electric warmth that tingle and awaken your whole body and your wolfish nature. You may feel sexually stimulated as well; this is a good sign.

Now, begin rhythmically up-growling with lips closed, so it will be more like a deep rumbling with each exhalation. Visualize the glowing wolf-power energy now filling, covering, and emanating from your entire body. Your whole extended aura is now glowing like a bright flame. When you have reached a state of empowerment, shift your low up-growl rumbling to low drawn-out up-howls every breath out. Your eyes should still be closed.

Call up your Animalself wolf by focusing your will as you continue to up-howl.

Using your combined focused will and your Animalself, make your glowing aura slowly shift into the form of a werewolf glowing like the sun. With your will and imagination, see yourself as a fiery werewolf. Push yourself, but don't strain. Let your Animalself do the work. Take your time. If you can't quite get it, end the practice and try another time. No worries—this is an exercise that can and should be repeated often as you like.

Once you have a clear image of yourself as a glowing werewolf in your mind, feel and see every part of it. Hold the image and feel the warming power as long as you can, a minute or two is great. Next, still breathing deeply and purposely, let the low howling die down and instead begin to growl the sound "HA" with each out-breath.

As you do so, your glowing werewolf form will come into more detailed focus as you exert your will for it to do so. It will shift from a glowing form to a "real" werewolf form with grey, black, or brown fur—whichever color you prefer. From our previous practices of calling forth our inner wolf, you'll know what your werewolf form looks like. Visualize this and will it as you continue the "HA" mantra.

In your mind's eye, visualize your fur, then bring into mental focus different parts of your werewolf form, working your way up your body. Silently say to yourself the following as you continue the exhaled "HA" mantra:

*I have the (*insert your chosen color*) hair of a wolf*
I have the paws of a wolf
I have the legs of a wolf
I have the loins of a wolf
I have the tail of a wolf …

Use this as you go on to visualize your chest, back, arms, head, fangs, claws, face, and ears changing. You are now a panting werewolf lying on the bed. Let the "HA" mantra fade. Keep your eyes closed as you visualize your werewolf body. Feel the physical strength of your werewolf body. Smell your fur and all the scents of the room. Taste the air around you. Listen: hear even the slightest sounds. Enjoy the feeling of being a werewolf. Be silent and relaxed.

When your focus begins to slip, end the exercise by reversing the process. Begin deep breathing and down-growling on out-breaths as before. Relax and let your werewolf form begin to glow and then dissolve into particles of light. With each in-breath, slowly pull the fiery energy back into your body. As you do so, let go of being a werewolf and shift your mind back to being a human. Shift your face, ears, and mouth back to your human form and so on, until you have shifted every body part back to human. Now you are just a glowing energized human.

Let your inner wolf withdraw back into your body, down into your inner mind. It is tired! Slowly withdraw the fiery extended wolf-power back into your gut center. Feel the warmth fade a bit as you see the tendrils of glowing energy withdraw until there is only the glowing wolf-power center. Lie still, relax, and be calm for a few minutes. Let things settle.

When you feel ready to end the practice, sit up slowly. Sprinkle salt water all over your body and the area around you to disperse the excess energy from the practice. There will be a lot of it! If it is your will, give thanks to the Lord of the Forest, the Moon Goddess, Gaia, and the Wolf Spirit with a long, simple, and quiet up-howl.

Wet the hand cloth with more of the salt water and wipe as much of your body as you can, including your hands, feet, and head. Later, pour out the last of the water outside by a tree. Write down your experiences and, if you choose, go to sleep. You will be tired. You may find yourself dreaming of loping over the hills in your wolf form! Do this practice regularly and your shape-shifting will improve in leaps and bounds.

The Praxis Shifting Rite

By this point, you are well practiced and proficient at the beginner Growl/Sway Exercise from chapter 3. Now it is time to level up to a more potent shape-shifting rite that is still simple, powerful, and effective.

The term praxis has two meanings that are both germane to this rite: the practical application of a theoretical idea and an accustomed or regular practice. It is being used here to remind you that this is a key rite that you will use many times from now on as part of shape-shifting rites, rituals, and spells. In a sense, this marks the beginning of real practical shape-shifting as opposed to preparing for it!

Throughout the rest of this book the Praxis Shifting Rite will often be used at the beginning of other rituals, spells, and so on to "kick start" them and you should be able to do this shifting rite well and with ease.

If you have become proficient with the previous Wolf-Power Exercise and the use of werewolf lingo, you will be able to pick this up easily. With practice, you will have powerful and surprising results. Once you're very familiar with it, feel free to creatively adapt and change elements of it as your Animalself inspires you.

This core rite is part of many werewolf magick rituals and spells. It can be done anytime and anywhere to enter a light werewolf trance for any purpose and works well to charge up other rituals. It would behoove you to learn it well and remember it.

A well-versed wer can do this in just a few minutes and "leave" the shift trance in the same amount of time. As you practice, pay attention to how it affects your body, your mind, your emotions, and your environment, including how others see you.

Setup

A full moon is best, especially when you are first learning, but any time that feels right for you is fine. Do this rite in a natural place with trees and somewhere you won't be disturbed; the wilder the better. Wear loose, relaxed clothing. Practicing this rite barefoot is best. It is powerful to do this rite just after doing the Wolf-Power Exercise because it supercharges this rite. I recommend that you try it with and without the Wolf-Power Exercise to see the difference. Find a comfortable spot to stand.

Items Needed

Your body, will, and mind

Some pure water to drink

The Rite

Begin by deep breathing, relaxing, and banishing all mental activity. Focus for a time on awakening your Animalself; see it as your inner wolf awakening, rising up, and filling you as your ego withdraws. Try to feel the wolf-power energy warmly spreading up and through your whole body. It will speed the awakening of your Animalself.

Visualize your full werewolf persona as clearly as you can. When you have a clear image of it, begin to sway side to side, foot to foot. Feel and vibrate to the now pulsing rhythm and the energy filling you from the earth.

Begin to low up-growl deep in your chest in rhythm to the rocking, much like you have done before. Close your eyes or keep them intentionally out of focus. Feel your werewolf form arise.

Begin up-growling the sound "HA" over and over in time with your swaying as you enter a trance. Go up slightly onto the balls of your feet and lean forward. Let your arms relax and open your shoulders, arms, and your chest. Raise your lupine head; splay your claws with arms outstretched.

Solidify the visualized shape-shift change to your werewolf form, from paws to crooked legs to loins to belly to chest to arms, head, face, and so on, as you have been practicing in the Wolf-Power Exercise.

Feel and "see" yourself growing larger and stronger as fur covers you. Add details, like your face extending into a fang-filled shout, claws and paws extending and your tail emerging. See and feel all this with absolute clarity as the astral energy solidifies.

As the visualized shift expands through your will and power, increase the volume and intensity of the rocking and growling "HA" mantra and feel the warmth fill and transform you completely as you become your inner wolf! Let your conscious mind and ego slide into the shadows and let your animal-self, your wolf mind, take over completely as you enter the trance state of being a wer.

Once the wolf mind is firmly in control and you can clearly feel and "see" yourself as the werewolf you want to be, slow the swaying and let the "HA" growling fade but continue to breathe deep. Go up on your paws; lean over, arms and claws outstretched. Bend your upper torso down with every out-breath. Reach with your claws and slowly bring them down while you visualize pulling down the power of the moon into your body. Slowly and intently down-howl as you do so.

Reach down and let your claws touch the earth. Visualize yourself pulling up the power of Gaia into your body and slowly and intently up-howl as you do so. Do this at least three or more times. The power you pull in to you will help solidify your astral and physical werewolf form.

When you feel fully werewolf, take a deep breath and just howl, no intonation, loud and proud! In this deeper trance state you are now in werewolf form and you are inflamed, filled with the fiery powers of the Wolf Spirit. At this point, you are now prepared to move on to any werewolf magick ritual or spell.

When you are ready to end the werewolf trance, raise your claws and up-howl three times to the moon, releasing all the excess astral lunar power you drew down from the Moon Goddess. Bend down and touch your claws to Gaia and down-howl three times, releasing all the excess earth power you drew down from Her.

Begin to sway back and forth again, but this time down-growl as you sway. Visualize and experience the transformation in reverse, slowly, step by step, beginning with mind, face, and head and then working down to your feet. At this point your werewolf form will contract and fade away with each sway.

Feel the fiery warmth of the wolf-power withdraw into your gut and fade to a small flame. Next, let the awakened Animalself wolf withdraw into your inner being as your human mind returns. Finally, visualize and feel your "normal" human body form return.

When you feel fully human, stomp your feet on the ground with several deep "MA" mantras. Do a full stretch, full intense body shake and bend down, placing your hands on the Earth. Say a silent thanks to the Lord of the Forest and to Gaia and release any excess energy with a long, exhaled growly "MA." Now, go forth as a recharged and wolfish human. Once you have practiced this rite a few times, feel free to alter it in a way that makes sense to your Animalself. There can be many variations of this rite by opening to the Wildness all about you and using it to empower this work. Be creative. Consult your inner wolf and have fun.

Wildness Shape-Shifting Ritual

As you move through this shape-shifting chapter, each practice and ritual will increase your shape-shifting game, expand your skills, and deepen your experiences by actually using the Wildness and your growing abilities to transform your being with the guidance of your Animalself. In this ritual you will expand and deepen your shape-shifting experiences by reaching out with your aura and tapping into the Wildness all about you in nature and using it to empower your work. Immersing yourself in the green power of Wildness and letting it flow through you is a key practice in werewolf magick and also promotes well-being. By also enhancing all senses, you will go even deeper into a liminal trance state and become more proficient at shape-shifting into a werewolf. The focus will be on inflaming your physical and psychic senses by enhancing them with the wolf-power to more intensely evoke your Animalself wolf form from the depths of the human body and assume it as a more confident werewolf.

This ritual is a step up from the last one but has similar patterns and steps. You will see that more is required of you and more will be expected in terms of shape-shifting. Each of the rituals presented is designed to move up a level while becoming more proficient at what has already been mastered, as with most disciplines.

How deeply, completely, and intensely this shape-shifting manifests is up to your desire, will, and focus. We are entering a stage where this process is becoming very potent magick. Though this is a ritual I have used with success, you are encouraged to adapt, alter, or shift things around as the inner voice of your Animalself suggests.

Just like the majority of our practices, this ritual is designed to be done out in the wilderness, but it doesn't have to be if safety or accessibility is an issue. Werewolf magick, although deeply connected with physical interactions with nature, can be done anywhere a natural environment has been created. If you do this ritual indoors, bring nature inside with you. Create as natural an environment as possible with living plants, forest images, bundles of fresh flowers and herbs, and so on; use your creativity. Werewolves, like all animals, adapt as they need to. If you are going to do the ritual inside, I'd suggest spending part of the day beforehand in nature and collecting some greenery to bring the aura of nature into your space. Finally, if you do opt for camping out in the wild, you need not do it alone. Others can be there for safety even if they are not participating.

Setup

This ritual should be done on or near a full moon in a natural area when there is warm and clear weather. A national forest or wilderness park would be ideal, but any private natural area with trees will work. Know where you're going; scout it out beforehand. You may choose to do this work for just a few hours or to camp overnight.

If you plan on camping, be prepared! Know what you are doing in terms of camping and have everything you will need for comfortably and safely camping out. You should be an experienced camper or with one. If you are planning to camp out, it would be best to find or reserve a campsite with a firepit so you can have a small fire.

Make sure the place is vibrant and attuned to the animal spirits. Locations near creeks are great. If you plan to do this ritual in a natural place without camping overnight, use a small red candle in a candle holder instead of a full fire and adjust the ritual accordingly. Make sure to have a container of water near the firepit or candle. Meditate deeply beforehand on your inner wolf. In your mind, try to clearly visualize what it looks like.

ITEMS NEEDED

If camping, appropriate camping gear and warm clothes so you're safe
   and healthy

Natural, loose, relaxing ritual clothing

Some cedar leaves or bark to burn (If cedar trees do not grow near you,
   use sage or rosemary.)

A bowl or dish to burn the leaves, bark, or herbs in

A stang and any other ritual tools you feel you will need

Healthy, raw food including, if it is your will, cold packed raw meat

Lots of water

A small clean washcloth

A werewolf magick talisman or belt

A werewolf anointing oil or salve dedicated to shifting

Simple foot gear aside from your normal footwear, such as sandals
   or moccasins, you will be wearing few or no clothes at times,
   but you want to protect your feet.

THE RITUAL

You should begin the ritual work by late afternoon, so plan accordingly to get to your campsite before then. Once you are there, set up an altar using a rock or log facing north and place the items you have brought on the altar. If you're doing this ritual indoors, any altar setup is fine.

Banish any extraneous energy by burning some cedar in your bowl or dish and circle your area counterclockwise. Up-growl nine times intensely, banishing all unwanted vibes and energies. Place the vessel of smoking cedar on the altar and pick up the stang. Walk around the whole area clockwise holding the stang, low up-howling three times as you go around. Visualize a green glowing circle form around you as the Lord of the Woods makes your space safe and powerful. When you're done, lean the stang upright against the altar or stick it into the ground.

Then, pray to the Moon Goddess, Gaia, and the werewolf gods for success with howls, growls, barks, and, if you like, a few growled words. Offer a few drops of water to them.

If you are camping out, set up camp and prep your fire, then relax and explore. Avoid speaking any human language. Meditate on the werewolf you will shift into. Clean up in a stream or with some of the water you brought with to cleanse yourself using the washcloth to do so, and then dry off. Eat as you need, but only raw, natural foods.

At twilight, light the fire (or candle) on the altar with a prayer for the success of this work using only howls, growls, barks. Put a little dry food on the altar in gratitude to the animal spirits, Gaia, the Lord of the Forest, the Moon Goddess, and other feral divine forces, as you will. If you're in the woods, bury the offering after your prayer. Then, sit and focus yourself. When centered, face the altar with the fire between you and it, then put some of the cedar bark or herbs into the fire. If you don't have a fire, burn some in the vessel on the altar. With your arms raised, utter a long, low up-howl to petition the spirits of this sacred place and to the werewolf powers to protect you from all dangers during this intense and personal endeavor. You are placing yourself into their hands. If you still have mundane clothing on, take the time to change into your clean, lose, and natural ritual clothing. Be still until you feel ready to begin calling forth the Lord of the Forest.

Stand up, put on your werewolf talisman, clap three times, then up-howl three times. Growl this invocation and visualize it clearly as it unfolds:

Twilight shadow
Emerge
From the deepest place

Into the silver
Glistening with gold
Eyes glowing green!
Now comes the horns
One in darkness, the other brilliant
The open eye
Where the horns meet opens.
Within your eye: a galaxy!
I see you!
Your nostrils flaring
Forest-filling grin
Lust, hunger, joy
And now you become as I become!!
A werewolf!
Bristling fur
Of shaggy forests
Hill-haunches
Wildness, Power, Ecstasy
Are mine and flow through me!
A meeting of all
A lightning bolt!
Join and aid me!
Together let us leap!
Dance! Play! Laugh!
Faunus Lycan
Come to me
Faunus Lycan
Set me free!
Faunus Lycan
So mote it be!

Now, loudly up-howl the sound "HA" three times, arms raised. Open all your senses! The Lord of the Forest will respond from without and within.

Be still! Feel the Wildness swirling about you, the breeze ruffling your hair-covered body. Smell the scents of the woods, so clear and powerful. Listen with more attuned ears and see with sharper eyes. Wait. The Lord of the Forest has many voices: some are silent, some are animal sounds or cries. The trees dance and mutter; the wind moans. Feel the rising wildness erupt within you and your hackles rise and flesh stir. I cannot say how the Lord of the Forest will reply to your call, but he will; be ready.

At this point, work on bringing forward the fiery wolf-power energy from your gut center as you have practiced in the previous Wolf-Power Exercise, but this time do the practice standing up. Feel the fiery wolf-power fill you and begin to transform you.

Shed as much of your human clothing as you feel comfortable. Being naked is best for this ritual, but if you keep some clothing on, it should be minimal, loose, and free. No matter what, put on the relaxed footwear you brought if you are outside. In front of the fire or candle, facing the altar, do the Praxis Shifting Rite. Feel the shifting happen as you slide into a deeper werewolf trance and as your inner wolf arises to the fore.

Rub the werewolf salve onto your body. You will do this one body part at a time while intensely visualizing your physical transformation and by growling the following phrase:

I have the paws of a wolf …
I have the crooked legs of a wolf …

… and so on until you reach your head, anointing each part as you go along.

As you rub the salve into your body, part by part, visualize fur sprouting, flesh and bone changing, and so on; will it to do so. Feel it, see it, experience the weaving of the internal trance state and Animalself integrating with your wolf-power-infused astral body helping to transform each part of your body. Concentrate on your sex, your heart, and your third eye.

Take your time; sip water as you need to. All your senses will wildly shift as you do this, so let yourself adjust. As you reach this stage of deep shape-shifting, your breathing will deepen. Let it become cycling, deep rumble-growls. Your stance is now utterly different—splayed, semi-crouched, clawed hands, standing on the balls of your feet.

Work on solidifying the shift when you are done with anointing yourself. Visualize your werewolf body as clearly as possible. Take your time; intensity in visualization is crucial now. What color is your fur? What exactly does each part of your werewolf form look like? Your wolfish eyes, ears, fangs, claws? Experience the transformation: your whole body and aura is tingling, glowing, changing. Continue to empower, focus, and solidify the glowing form of your werewolf self with the wolf-power drawn from your glowing gut center. Bring that form into focus and feel the truth of this experience. Finally, center your werewolf form until you feel, see, and know you are a full werewolf.

When the shape-shifting feels complete, you will experience a sudden rush and a kind of "click" as your human mind becomes silent. The Animalself rules now. Your senses will change; they will be heightened. You will smell numerous scents you did not smell previously. Your night sight will become clearer, less about color and more about accuracy. All your senses will increase in intensity. Water tastes amazing, you feel every breeze intensely, and hear every rustle of the trees. Your environment is suddenly alive to you! Smell it. Feel it. Taste it. See it. Hear the many small sounds around you. Enjoy the feeling of being a werewolf!

Luxuriate in the beauty and power of your shifted werewolf form. Continue and increase your rumbly growl-breathing; make it more intense and deeper and more purposeful. Then change it to a repetitive growly "HA" with each out-breath.

Your werewolf body is now bigger, stronger, and more powerful than it was the last time you tried shifting because the Wildness is now attuned to you and you to it. As you energize it, your "HA … HA … HA" growl-breathing will shift to louder up-growls. Prowl around the circle as you do this, enjoying the feeling of your new werewolf body.

When you feel your shape-shift is at a clear peak, loudly up-howl with your whole body in front of the altar while burning the image of yourself as this beautiful, powerful werewolf into your mind. Follow this howl with a moment of letting loose. Leap, prowl, dance, lope, howl, yip, and bark around the area, around the fire if you have one burning. Literally *go wild!* Enjoy the freedom of being a full werewolf! Dance, play, and revel as you like! Take breaks to drink some water as well. Explore this new world as you like. You'll be surprised at what you will hear, see, and smell now in your werewolf form.

When you're hungry, pounce on, and devour the raw food, then offer some to the gods and spirits with up-growls and barks, either on your altar or thrown into your fire.

Being a newbie wer, at some point the stress of holding this trance state will tug on you physically. When you feel that tug, it's time to reverse the shift. To start the reverse, hold both paws to your solar plexus to feel and center the fiery werewolf-power you have stoked there. With deep breathing and low down-growls, pull the energy filling your body slowly out of your limbs; see and feel it flow back to the fire center, into your paws. As it withdraws, down-growl "MA" over and over, letting go. As you do this, feel the elation, energy, and power withdraw as your werewolf self, in a sense, deflates.

Now, release the shifting trance. Begin to rhythmically stomp on the ground, alternating paws, while still continuing the "MA" down-growls. Let the werewolf power and your werewolf self dissolve in sparks of light as the excess energy flows down into the earth, into Gaia. At the same time, release your wolf mind and let it sink back into your inner mind, see your Animalself curl up in your inner mind as your human consciousness arises and awakens.

Slowly return to your human form … close your eyes … let your body and mind alter and adjust. Remove the werewolf belt or talisman and rub it on every part of your body, just as you anointed yourself earlier, beginning with your feet and ending by rubbing your head, third eye, and crown. See the lingering wolf-power being absorbed into this item. As you finish, growl-whisper three times:

Werewolf I was,
Human I am
So mote it be
I am again me.

At this point you have finished shifting every body part back to being human. You are now human: physically, energetically, and psychologically. Pick up your talisman or belt and wave it about you in a clockwise direction and silently give thanks to the Lord of the Forest. Touch the talisman to the earth and silently thank Gaia. Touch it lightly to the fire or the candle flame and silently thank the animal spirits and your own Animalself. Go to the altar and hang the talisman or belt on the stang. Drink and offer a few drops of water at the altar and then blow out the candle if you have one. If you have a fire, put more cedar into the fire (or light more in the vessel) to purify yourself and the area with the smoke while doing nine final up-growls to finish the ritual.

Write down all your experiences in your journal. While you'll be excited, you will also be worn out and should get some sleep. Write down your dreams when you awake. After you have done this ritual with success a few times, you will be ready for full werewolf shifting, a kind of initiation and werewolf magick shape-shifting graduation.

Advanced Wildness Shape-Shifting Ritual

In this ritual you will take practical werewolf shape-shifting to a much more intense level. Consider this your advanced werewolf shape-shifting initiation. You are moving forward with your shape-shifting skills, they are becoming second nature and now you are upping your game. While this ritual is similar to the ones we've already practiced, this ritual builds upon what is becoming second nature now and pushes the shifting ability to get you to magickally and personally exceed what you have already accomplished as well as intensify the power and flow of your Animalself. The Animalself thrives on our will, desire, and embrace of the physical self, all of which will get stronger here. Once you have mastered this, you will be able to go on to evolve, change, and implement your own shape-shifting practices and create your own rituals and experiences with your inner wolf to guide you. This is just the beginning.

To hone your skills, practice the previous rituals in this chapter several times, get better and more powerful, then take shape-shifting as far as you can with this ritual.

Setup

As with the previous ritual, this ritual is intended to be done in the wilderness, but as has been previously noted, it need not be done that way. Werewolf shifting can be conjured within any natural environment. This ritual would be most powerful if it's done at a full or near full moon, on a clear and very warm night. Similar to the last ritual, if you are able to practice this outside, try to reserve a campsite with a fire ring and that is isolated from other humans. Know where you're going to go, scout it out beforehand, and, if you are camping overnight, make sure you have all the necessary gear. You will be in a deep trance state once the ritual really gets going, so make sure to be extra organized and careful in your prep. Meditate deeply beforehand on your inner wolf and what *you* look like as a werewolf.

Items Needed

Be prepared with all needed camping gear like a tent, sleeping bag, tools, and so on.

All natural, loose clothing

Sandals or other minimal footwear, aside from your walking or hiking shoes

Plenty of fresh water, raw and natural food such as meat (cooked or raw), nuts, veggies, fruit, and so on

The stang, a cup, your knife, and any other tools you wish to bring

Dried rosemary, sage, cedar leaves, or bark

Brandy or rich red wine (or other ceremonial beverage)

A special, comfy, all-wool ritual blanket

A red candle and candle holder if you will not have a campfire

A blessed werewolf belt or talisman

A sacrament that your Wolf Spirit has directed you to bring

A totemic wolfish item or image that the Wolf Spirit has directed you to bring

Ritual werewolf shape-shifting salve you've created

Dark chocolate

THE RITUAL

Begin the ritual just as twilight begins so there is light to see. Most of the items you will need are the same as the previous ritual, with the addition of a few other items. However, feel free to bring along whatever you think you might need. After doing the previous ritual, you may have some good ideas about what you'll need, including other camping gear and tools. You can do this at the same site if you like. Know your wilderness area well. Make sure to choose an area that is clearly defined so you will not get lost because you will be night prowling in a deep werewolf trance. Check the place out in full daylight and wander about the area where you will be doing this ritual so you'll know it. Use urine, just like a wolf would, to mark around your "territory."

Set up your campsite like you did in the previous Wildness Shape-Shifting Ritual. Make sure to have a container of water near the firepit or candle.

Place the herb you're using in the burning vessel and light it, then cleanse and purify your area with the smoke by carrying it around your campsite counterclockwise, up-growling loudly while visualizing the unwanted energies flying away.

Set up an altar facing north like you did for the previous ritual, using a stone, log, or stump as you like. Place a branch of any appropriate leafy or conifer tree on it. Set the stang upright, either leaning on the altar or stuck in the ground upright behind it. Lay out the cup, knife, and all other tools you have. Pour wine into the cup.

Take up the vessel of burning herb again. Honor the Moon Goddess, Gaia, and the Lord of the Forest by doing the following: low up-howl and hold the smoking herb up to the moon, then low up-howl and lower the smoking herb down towards the earth, then honor the Lord of the Forest by low up-howling and walking with the smoking herb in a clockwise circle about your area. Visualize white light seeping from the forest and filling your circle and you.

Next, bring the smoking herb and set it on the altar and growl any prayers from the heart while offering herb smoke and some wine from the cup to the great Wolf Spirit and the Animalself within you, as well as to the spirits of the wilderness. Drink some of the wine with some up-growls and a howl. Get in the mood, open your arms, and embrace all of nature, the gods, spirits, and the ever-present wolf-power. Ask for success, protection, and guidance with three barks, a long up-howl, and a bit of wine poured out onto the altar. Fill the cup back up with wine for later.

Place the folded wool blanket you brought with before the altar. Sit there, relax, and meditate on all you did before, on the ritual, on your werewolf form, and on your determination to take the shape-shifting further this time. Also meditate on the concepts of Wildness, Wyrd, and Way, opening yourself to each of these powers and letting them enter and flow through you.

As you do so, breathe deeply and rhythmically, add rumble growling, and open yourself completely and calmly to nature. Focus on the Wildness and the Instinct flowing through you from your lower body up to your center. Then focus on the Wyrd that weaves all things with inspiration glowing at your heart. Finally, open your third eye center and accept the insights filling you as you stop your internal chatter and open to the Way of all. Be silent.

At this point twilight is deepening, so arise and start a fire in the fire pit, making sure you have enough kindling and firewood to keep it burning as long as you'll need it. Be silent.

When you are ready to begin the shape-shifting, throw some of the herb in the fire and up-howl three long, slow "HA" sounds. Then, take off as much clothing as you are comfortable with. Being naked is best for this ritual, but whatever you keep on should be minimal, loose, and free. No matter what you decide on for clothing, put on the relaxed footwear you brought to protect your feet. Continue to low up-howl "HA" while you stretch, shake, and awaken your Animalself, which at this point, with all your practice, should be able to arise quickly and easily.

Empower your sacred space by facing north, raise your hands up, and call the wolf-power by up-howling. While deeply up-howling, lope about the circumference of the circle three times. End it at the altar with a long, full exhalation and in a growly voice say, "Haaaaaaaaa..." Touch the earth, feel its strength and its roots.

Call all the wolf-power you have ever generated into your being from the four directions with the power of your will and love. Face each direction, hold your arms up and vibrate while vocalizing, "HA." Hold your arms straight up, focusing on the stars, and vibrate "HA" toward the full moon. Touch your paws to the earth and vibrate "HA" to Gaia. Finally, inhale "HA'" and absorb and become one with the collected Wolf Spirit energy. Let it fill you!

At this point, start doing the Wolf-Power Exercise. Evoke the wolf-power energy from your gut center as you have practiced previously. Feel it fill you and begin to transform you. As you do the fiery Wolf-Power Exercise like you've practiced before, add a few new steps: As the wolf-power fills your whole body, see it glow especially bright in your lower body. Up-howl "HA," calling to the Wildness to enhance your animal instincts. Then see the wolf-power glow especially bright in your chest. As you up-howl "HA," call to the Wyrd to enhance your deep awareness of the Wyrd that weaves you and nature as one. See the wolf-power glow especially bright red, shining forth from your third eye. As you up-howl "HA" a final time, connect with the Way of all things in silence.

Once you are a fully flaming energetic werewolf form, up-howl with all your energy. In front of or next to the fire, facing the altar, do the Praxis Shifting Rite. Most likely the shape-shifting will happen much faster and deeper than before as you slide into a deeper werewolf trance. Your Animalself wolf has already filled you by now and will easily slide into the driver's seat. You will feel waves of rushing energy, so breathe deeply, sway, and let it flow through you as the shifting accelerates.

Put on your werewolf talisman or belt and growl this adapted traditional werewolf invocation:

Spirits of the Night
Be kind to me!
Spirits of the Moon and Stars
Be kind to me!
Spirits of the Trees and Rocks,
Streams and Plants
Be kind to me!
Spirits of the Animal Ancestors,
Now and in the Past
Within and Without

Be kind to me!
Oh Spirit of the Beasts
Be kind to me!
Oh Wolf-Self!
Let me take your form
Let me run, stalk, play, and love
In your sacred form!
By the Power of the Secret Wild Lord!
Io An!

As the energies swirling through and about you stabilize and settle, begin deep breathing and low-growling "HA" repeatedly. Take up the werewolf salve, rub some on your sex, heart, and third eye centers and throw some into the fire with a howl.

Now, begin to thoroughly rub the werewolf salve onto your body like you did with the previous ritual, doing so one body part at a time, while intensely visualizing and evoking your physical transformation. At this point you are beyond human words, so with pure instinct rub each part while continuing to down-growl "HA" deeply. You will see and feel the physical shift of each part of your body as you do so. Do this slowly and intensely with no conscious intellect, beginning with your foot paws and ending with the furry crown of your head. Take your time, make it real, and push further into the shape-shift trance and transformation than before. Visualize and feel the change intensely. When it feels right, let the "HA" growling fade.

When you are fully shape-shifted and standing tall in full werewolf form, begin to move. Prowl about the ritual area clockwise, deep down-growling rhythmically. Get used to your werewolf body and mind, revel in being a wer. Do this as long as you wish, until your werewolf consciousness and deep trance state is in full control.

When you are fully shifted and feel the wolf-power erupting through you, do a full-body howl. Leap up with claws reaching to the full moon and emit a long explosive "HA" that becomes a wild scream. Then do a series of wild, full-body howls that obliterate the last of your human mind. You are a werewolf now. Prowl over to the altar and drink some of the sacrament your werewolf consciousness has indicated.

Now that you have fully shifted into a werewolf, let the powers you've invoked fill you and let the wolf's sacrament enhance the process; stay focused, your Animalself rules.

When it feels right, drag the blanket in front of the fire if you have one or stay in front of the altar. Crouch, sit, or lie upon the blanket. Put your sandals by the blanket. Let the wolf-power wash over, through you, and fill you with the pure Wildness. No more words. Growl, yip, howl, or be silent.

Let your wild werewolf sex instinct rise from your loins like a flame within your powerful furry body and begin self-love. Focus on the moon. You are making love with the Wildness, Wyrd, and Way, with all of nature, then with the werewolf goddesses or gods. Let the experience consist purely of animal senses and pleasure, no human words or thoughts. Your energy should feel like wolves mating in primal heat and lust. Upon climax, howl with every fiber of your werewolf being. You and your Animalself have merged; you are completely a werewolf now. Hold that animal bliss as long as you can. Rub the fluids into your head fur, chest fur, on all your limbs and belly fur, your third eye, and every other part of your werewolf body to seal the shape-shifting.

At this point, operate on pure instinct; you are fully feral, go where it takes you. Squat, sniff the rich air, enjoy being a beast! When the mood takes you, put on your sandals and go prowling into the darkness as a werewolf. Don't forget to stay within sight of your fire. Go into the shadows of the wilderness, into the wild darkness and pause.

Sniff the air and smell the forest and animal trails. Listen to the nighttime sounds and the wind: feel the bark on trees, the moist earth. Be open and exalt in all your now-expanded senses! Feel your new body, paws, fur, and fangs. What a glorious feeling!

When acclimated to this new sensory awareness and animal consciousness, carefully wander. Lope! Prowl! Crawl! Stalk!

Creep up on small nocturnal animals, but let them be. You will scare them!

Avoid but watch the larger ones with your enhanced werewolf vision. Stop, lie against a tree: really listen and feel! Listen to all the spirits; as a wer you are welcome here and now deeply connected with these ancient and wise beings.

If there is a creek, feel the chilly water, listen to the sounds and voices. Open your third eye and see the power spots and the ley lines of energy all about you. This is a glimpse of the Wyrd. Free of human ego, you now can access all your lower cortex Animalself abilities and there is so much to see, feel, and experience! Explore with joy and do so wordlessly. Growl, yip, bark, and howl as you prowl and play.

When you are tired or feel the tug of your human-self, return to your circle. Warm yourself by the fire. Wrap a blanket about you if needed or dress in your loose clothing. Drink water and some wine or brandy and offer some to Gaia, the Moon Goddess, the Lord of the Forest, and any other spirits. Wordlessly up-growl and up-howl thanks. Hang out and chill as long as you can in this werewolf form.

When you feel the trance and wolf-power beginning to subside, it is time to leave the werewolf state. Breathe deeply and slowly begin to come back into your human-self, beginning with low down-growling "HA" over and over again. As you do so, place your paws on your head and withdraw all the wolf-power into your third eye. Continue down-growling "HA" over and over again, moving your hands and the power downward. Move your paws down to your heart and withdraw all the fiery wolf-power down from your head and from your arms and torso into your heart. Finally, moving the power and hands downward, place your paws on your lower gut, the wolf-power center, and withdraw all the wolf-power from your chest, belly, loins, and legs until all the wolf-power sinks back into the gut-fire center.

As it withdraws, continue down-growling "HA" but softer and softer, slowly letting go. As you do this, feel the elation, energy, and power withdraw as your werewolf self, in a sense, deflates. Place your hands on the earth and down-growl "MA" three times and let the excess energy sink into Gaia.

Stand and begin to rhythmically stomp on the ground, alternating your feet while keeping a beat with repeated "MA" down-growls. Let the last werewolf power, the trance state, and werewolf energy flow down into the earth, into

Gaia. At the same time, release your Animalself to sink back into your deep self and visualize it curling up in your inner mind as your human conscious-ness slowly arises and awakens.

As you slowly return to your human-self, close your eyes, let your body and mind alter and adjust as you silently breathe deeply. Remove the werewolf belt or talisman and rub it on every part of your body as before, the way you anointed yourself earlier, ending with rubbing your third eye and crown. See the lingering wolf-power being absorbed into and charging this item. To affirm you are human again, growl-whisper:

Werewolf I was,
Human I am
So mote it be
I am again me

Toss more herb on the fire or burn it in the vessel on the altar as an offer-ing of thanks and bathe in the smoke to purify yourself with long, low down-growls. Relax. Be. Feel the deep joy of being one with all Wildness as you return to being almost fully human, though you never will be again. Chill, meditate, and rest. Come back to yourself, but remain quiet, no words. Dress if you are chilly. Eat some food and hydrate. Then have some wine or brandy and eat the chocolate; it really helps earthing. Sleep when and as you like.

The next day, place the herb in the burning vessel and light it. Cleanse and purify your area with the herb smoke, up-growlng loudly nine times while visualizing all excess energies flying away as you walk around your area coun-terclockwise. Clear off the altar and put away your tools, but leave some of your raw food on it as an offering and quietly up-howl thanks to all the deities and spirits you have been calling on. Finally, crouch or lie on the earth; feel the power of Gaia rise up and embrace you. You are one of her wild children now. Then quietly growl:

HA
To you

From you
All things
MA

If you're camping out, stay as long as you like in that lovely wild area; take a long hike the next day. At some point, record all your experiences in your journal. Make sure to write or draw the flood of ideas, information, and dreams that came to you. When you do leave, go forth as you will with a wild joy in your heart. Offer a quiet howl-prayer for the freeing of all people from their civilized prisons. Don't forget to leave the site as you found it; a good wolf is an eco-friendly wolf.

Practice, Practice, Practice

Well done! You have successfully worked through the core practices of werewolf shape shifting. Pause for a moment and realize that this is just the beginning of your successes. You have begun the process of becoming a werewolf and now know the basics, but you have not mastered the process as well as you can. Yet. As with any crucial task, skill or practice, multiple successes build and deepen proficiency, skill and intensity. This is why you will want to practice the shape-shifting you've done multiple times before moving on to the work of creating a Fetch. In this way you'll get better, go deeper and shift more intensely. Letting the full Animalself really manifest takes time and effort, like anything else, but it is worth it in terms of both empowering and improving all your other werewolf magick, spells, and rituals.

CHAPTER 6

FETCH WORK

———————— ╫ ————————

In this chapter we're going to take some time to learn more about our Double and how it can be used by you in werewolf magick as your own personal separate wolfish entity, which we'll be calling a Fetch. You will see that your own werewolf magick Fetch can be used in a number of very practical ways. Before we dive in, let's do a quick review on the idea behind the Double and how it can be made into a Fetch.

The Double is a separate spiritual entity from our soul, recognized by ancient and current cultures. In other spiritual and occult systems it is sometimes called the astral or etheric body. In that sense, it is a spiritual part of each of us that can independently travel out of the body and, through will, travel the physical and astral or spiritual worlds. This astral Double can be strengthened with magick and re-formed into any aspect the person wills through focus and magick, in our case that of a wolf or werewolf. The Double is one of the things we have been working on and energizing. It is the key to the shape-shifting we have accomplished already as we become werewolves. Building on the shape-shifting we've practiced so far, we will take this aspect of astral shape-shifting further.

As you read earlier in the book in the Invoking or Calling Down Divine Powers section of chapter 2, our Double can also be projected outward, not just expanded within us. It can function as a vehicle for our consciousness or as a separate entity with some magick. Our work with the wolf-power has strengthened our Double, which we shaped into a wolf or werewolf form with a lot of directed will and energy. It is this energetic form we evoke and "wear" to shape-shift, but now we can see that a lot of what we have been doing also has been empowering our Animalself to the point where our Animalself, in the form of a wolf, and our Double *have become one and the same.* We can work with it internally or externally, as without, so within.

Now that we have connected the dots and mastered shape-shifting, let's look at what our Double can do when we evoke and project it as an external entity. To make things clearer when discussing this entity, we will call this external Double by one simple term: Fetch.

We have learned about evoking and invoking and can now see that these practices reinforce and combine in werewolf magick. Once we evoke, externalize, and empower our Fetch, we can project that same Fetch as a separate spirit or entity. We can invoke it at will as a separate spirit and work with it in many ways.

Your Double is very flexible. Projecting and working with it as a Fetch will not interfere with your shape-shifting work, but you will likely need to focus on one or the other at any given time, for shape-shifting is internal and Fetch work is external.

Invoking the Fetch in Werewolf Magick

We have already done most of the work with our Animalself needed to begin to externalize it as a Fetch, so much of the following process shouldn't be too surprising. We focus on, connect with, and externalize our Fetch as an astral wolf or werewolf spirit that can leave the physical body. This is done through meditation, ritual, and energized enthusiasm. This Fetch is visualized, manifested, and treated as an external spirit that has the form of a wolf spirit or werewolf. This is done by using the practices you have already been doing, such as the Praxis Shifting Rite, the Wolf-Power Exercise, and other shape-shifting techniques. The only real difference is that Fetch work is about doing all this to empower the Fetch as an external spiritual being, not for personal shape-shifting.

Once our Double is empowered and evoked this will be breathing life into it as a Fetch. When it is perceived, fully accepted, and we have bonded with it, we can then work with it as traditional witches would. We can petition, honor, and invoke the Fetch as a spirit or demon, though it is fashioned of our own astral body, our Double.

Once we successfully invoke our werewolf Fetch as an external being, there are many possibilities. We can communicate with it and ask for guidance and advice through divination, telepathy, or visions. Being the externalized werewolf spirit of our deepest primal being, it has access to our unconscious mind and it contains information our conscious self does not.

Some of the old witchcraft trial documents relate that witches "rode wolves or werewolves to the sabbat." Now that we have succeeded in shape-shifting and "wearing the wolf skin'" we can externalize this "wolf skin" as the Fetch and, like these witch ancestors, ride this astrally empowered werewolf spirit form on the astral plane.

The externalized Fetch, visualized and invoked as a vehicle of werewolf projection, can be used in two ways: We can take all we've learned and experienced and apply it to simple Fetch work, such as riding the Fetch in dreams or out in the world. We can also apply our knowledge and skills and do complex Fetch work where we feed and work with the Fetch as a spirit that will protect and do things for us. As such, the Fetch becomes what witches would call a Familiar. Think of all this as externalized shape-shifting of your astral body. Our first step to doing this work is to call forth and reify our Fetch.

Calling Forth and Shape-Shifting the Fetch Exercise

The first step in calling forth the Fetch is bringing forth from within us our Double as an external Fetch. We will use the same belief, power, and astral intensity we've practiced to the point where it is seen, visualized, and manifested as a living, semi-independent spiritual entity. In werewolf magick, the Fetch may be manifested as a powerful large wolf or as a werewolf, which completely depends on what seems natural for you.

SETUP

Make sure you have read and understand everything about the Double and Fetch. Meditate on why you want to pursue this particular aspect of werewolf magick. Read through the exercise that follows and think on it. While you are contemplating these ideas, find a natural place with trees and good energies to practice this work. This work is strongest if you are able to do it barefoot.

ITEMS NEEDED

Relaxed, natural clothing

Your werewolf talisman

THE EXERCISE

Banish and center your space as you like. One simple way to do this is to up-growl nine times counterclockwise and see all other energies fading away. Once your space feels ready, do the Praxis Shifting Rite, put on your werewolf talisman, and then follow those steps with the Wolf-Power Exercise.

Now, hold out your hands and cup them in front of you. As a fiery wer, low up-howl several times, and call forth your Double from your fiery werewolf self as a glowing ball of energy. Keep low up-howling and focusing your will and fiery werewolf power on this ball of energy. Let it flow out of you and into this glowing ball until you see and feel the Fetch as a separate being of energy in your cupped hands. You will sense it beginning to awaken.

Change your up-howls to low down-howls and as you do so, let your entire werewolf form, power, and being flow into this "energy ball" you are holding. As you do this, you will transfer all the fiery energy and your werewolf-ness to this entity energy ball.

It will grow, glow, and become more distinct and aware. It will likely change form, color, and so on. Focus your will intensely and with every out-breath, down-growl "HA" over and over.

As you do this, the Fetch will be absorbing all of the wolf-power from you, to the point that you will naturally start returning to human form and consciousness. While still cupping the now distinct and aware Fetch in your hands, begin to sway and stomp your feet with the same down-growl "HA" sounds. You'll begin to feel yourself returning to your human state as your Fetch consumes all your werewolf energy. When you fully return to being human and the Fetch is clearly present and awake, pause in silence. Low-growl "HA" three times loudly and see the Fetch come into focus, likely as a small glowing wolf or werewolf.

After a time, reach out to your Fetch with your human mind and make sure it is full of kindness and love. Treat it as you would a new puppy. At this point, you may sit and relax but continue to cradle the new Fetch. Take this time to ask it a very important question telepathically: What is its name and symbol?

Once you have this information, you are ready to go further. Thank and bond with the Fetch for a bit; you'll be tired since you "fed" it with your energy.

When you feel ready, bring the glowing Fetch up to your talisman or let the talisman fall onto the Fetch. Welcome and nudge the Fetch by growling its name it gave you, visualize its symbol glowing over the talisman, and cajole it into the talisman. This is where it will live unless you give it another physical "lair." See it enter the talisman and the power die down as it sleeps.

Then, touch the earth with your hands, down-growl "MA" three times, and let all the excess energy from the work flow into the earth. Stand and up-howl three times, thanking the Moon Goddess who rules the astral world, the Lord of the Forest who rules animal spirits, and Gaia who is all of nature. You have now successfully shape-shifted and manifested your externalized werewolf Fetch!

Building Up the Fetch Exercise

The more intention, will, and energy you pour into your Fetch, the more useful it will be. In werewolf magick, this is called "feeding" the Fetch. Once you have conjured and bonded with it, you will want to work with it. Again, think of it as a new puppy. If you conjure it and then ignore it, your Fetch will wander off. Who wouldn't? Focus, intention, will, and love are the keys to any serious magick and will empower and keep your Fetch a separate entity that can evolve.

Setup

Practice this exercise in a natural place with trees. As usual, real wilderness is best, but make do with whatever access you have. Make sure to have done the previous ritual before doing this one. It is best if you have done it several times successfully. Meditate on why you are doing this and what you wish to do with your Fetch. This exercise requires, well, exercise, both mental and physical. Have a plan and way to do some real exercise, such as fast walking, jogging, hiking, or even weightlifting or yoga. It should be somewhat strenuous and energetic; do what you are able to do. Take some time to review the Wolf-Power Exercise before you begin.

Items Needed

Lose, relaxed exercise clothing

Your werewolf talisman

Some fresh drinking water

The Exercise

When you get to the natural place you have chosen, put your werewolf talisman on and then banish unwanted energies with nine up-growls as you turn counterclockwise. You may also use werewolf lingo to call to and honor the werewolf gods and spirits as you will. Once you feel ready, do the Praxis Shifting Rite. Feel and activate your wolf-power and let the fiery energy expand and fill you from your solar plexus out, but do this silently and quickly without actually taking on the full fiery werewolf form. Hold the increased wolf-power in your body.

At this point, do your physical exercise with gusto! Build up your physical energy and push your intellect and thinking mind to the side. As you exercise, silently call your Fetch by its name and visualize its symbol glowing on your talisman and quietly up-growl "HA" over and over until it appears this time as a separate entity floating before you. Quietly up-howl three times in greeting.

Increase your exercise and as you do so, feed the energy you're generating directly into the Fetch. As you do so, your Fetch will become clearer and clearer, more in focus as a definite being, and will look intently at you, happy at being fed. Remember to think of your Fetch as a new puppy.

Keep exercising and begin to silently chant the name of your Fetch over and over until you get tired and your exercise session slows and stops. When you're done exercising, sit quietly and drink water, all the while focusing your will, love, and energy on the Fetch, who is soaking it up. Honor and bond with your Fetch as you feed it with all the energy you generated while exercising. As you do so, see the image of the Fetch get clearer and larger. Hold this image in your mind.

With several low down-growl "HA" sounds, silently commune with it, praise it, listen to it, and then thank it, using its name. Finally, dismiss it by holding out your talisman and inviting it to enter its home. When it has done so, sit and qui-

etly down-growl "MA," then stand and gently stomp on the ground while swaying a bit until you are back to your full human-self and out of the trance state.
Thank the gods and goddesses as you like with three low up-howls, ground the
excess energy by touching the earth and giving it to Gaia, then go take a shower!

You may do this exercise as often as you like depending on how much time
and energy you want to invest in your Fetch. As with anything, the more effort
you put into this work, the greater the success. Instead of exercise, you may do
any similar energy generating activity, like using orgasm energy from self-love
or intensely doing art.

Exercise to Create a Fetch Shrine

So far your talisman has been the place where your Fetch lives when you are not
calling upon it. However, when you are able to call upon your werewolf Fetch
easily and can bring it to you quickly with its name and symbol, you will see
that it has grown and become more substantial. Your Fetch "puppy" will have
matured and grown, evolving into a full, more independent wolf spirit entity.
With its growth, you will need to create and dedicate a larger home for it.

SETUP

Now is the time to decide how much you want to work with your Fetch on a
regular basis. If you are committed to an ongoing relationship with your Fetch,
you may want to create a small shrine for it in your home or yard. Before com-
mitting to a shrine, you'll need to have a strong bond with your Fetch and a
very clear image of what it looks like, as well as the name and symbol. Before
starting this exercise, decide on where you want the shrine to be and where
you want to create it. This will be something of an occult "craft" project, as
you'll see.

ITEMS NEEDED

A small wooden box or "shrine" you buy or make. A small wooden birdhouse
can be adapted easily.
Any natural art materials you need to create an image or icon of what your
Fetch looks like. Clay or small pieces of board and paints, whatever you feel
is right. One idea is to find a small smooth stone onto which you write or

draw the Fetch's name and symbol. Keep in mind that the image has to fit into a small space.

Permanent markers, red and black

Some shape-shifting werewolf salve you have been using

Your werewolf magick talisman

A small bowl or plate for offerings to the Fetch

Some pure water and some natural food that isn't messy,
    such as nuts or berries.

A red flower

An oak leaf or any other leaf you feel is right

THE EXERCISE

Assemble all the items you need at your desk or table. Banish the area of unwanted energies with nine up-growls as you turn counterclockwise. Then do the Praxis Shifting Rite. Up-howl low and in a friendly way three times, visualizing your Fetch and its symbol and calling it to you. It will come to you quickly at this point if you have been working with it regularly; you are its parent after all! When it appears and you feel its presence, utter low up-howls and silently communicate with your Fetch.

Silently tell it you are building it a shrine, a Fetch house, and will feed it regularly, but that you will want it to work harder with you and for you. Close your eyes and visualize it glowing before you. Focus intently on the image of your werewolf Fetch. If it clearly agrees to this simple pact, then you are ready.

In a trance, create the icon or image of your Fetch while low growling its name over and over. Make sure the icon includes the Fetch's symbol on it. Create and decorate the interior and exterior of this Fetch shrine. Again, make sure the symbol the Fetch gave you is on the shrine.

When you're done decorating the icon and the shrine, anoint the icon image of your Fetch with some of the werewolf shape-shifting salve, quietly up-howl "HA" three times, and see your Fetch enter the now-sacred icon. Growl-whisper its name to the image three times, and growl chant:

Oh thou Fetch who art of me
My love and will I give to Thee
Do my bidding, protect and see
With love and will, so mote it be.

Touch the icon or image to the werewolf talisman and hang the talisman on the shrine. Then, place the icon or image in the shrine, bless and honor your Fetch with love and werewolf lingo as you will, and then feed it by placing the small plate in front of or in the shrine with some nuts or berries, the red flower, and the oak leaf or leaf of your choice. Paint a circle of love and protection on and around the shrine, clockwise, with some of the werewolf salve. Do this while low down-howling, thus blessing and sealing it.

When you're done, leave your werewolf trance state as per the Praxis Shift Rite and let all the excess energy flow down into the earth. Place your hands on the shrine and down-howl "MA" to thank Gaia for this blessing. The shrine can now be moved to its permanent location, either inside or outside.

Feeding the Fetch Regularly

Once the Fetch is "installed" in its shrine and placed where it will live, begin to feed your Fetch at least once a week. Do simple devotions in front of the shrine like so:

Do the Growl/Sway Exercise in front of the shrine and call the Fetch forth, then pour some of your werewolf energy into your Fetch. It will be happy being fed. Use any werewolf lingo you wish, and commune with it. Give it offerings of simple food and/or flowers or leaves, depending on what feels right to you and what your Fetch asks for.

When you are done and your Fetch is ready to rest in its new home, sit and quietly down-growl "MA" until it is settled in and until you are back to full human form, consciousness, and out of that light trance state. Thank the gods and goddesses as you like with a low up-howl and ground the excess energy by touching the earth and giving it to Gaia.

In the future you can offer your Fetch all kinds of things that will add to its power, including sexual energy and fluids, or any other items that feel right to you. Some old Witchcraft practices say a Fetch (a Familiar if you're a witch) should be fed with a bit of your blood regularly, but that is up to you and what feels right for your practice.

Whether you work with your Fetch seldom or often, having this werewolf magick ally is very useful. It can be called upon for any astral work such as distance viewing, protection, and to aid in shape-shifting. You can consult with it, or "ride it" in dreams or on astral adventures. You also can request deeper werewolf magick teachings or ask it to do things for you, such as "fetching" or manifesting items you need. As you read the werewolf magick spells coming up later in the book, consider how your Fetch could enable, empower, or help carry out your spells. It can help and guard you in any number of psychic endeavors.

Sleep Fetch Work Exercise

Working with your Fetch in a dream is the fastest and most efficient way to bond with it and get to know this spirit/part of yourself. As you continue to feed and work with your werewolf Fetch, the mental and astral image of it as an external entity should become clearer and clearer until it can be easily conjured to your inner eye. Dreamtime is the liminal place where you and your Fetch can directly meet and communicate and become closer. Once this happens, you'll be able conjure your Fetch in this world very easily. Spending time with your Fetch in dreams and real life is powerful magick. The multi-level visualization, conjuring, and invocation of the Fetch will build its powers and it will become more useful in your dreams, on the astral plane, and in the real world.

Setup

Once you are at a place where your Fetch is a very real part of your world and you are able to clearly visualize and connect with it, you are ready to do dream work with it. This work can be done in your bed or, if you wish, while camping. This exercise works best if you're naked, but do whatever is comfortable for you. Make sure your space or room is completely clean, organized, and aired out. Moon power deeply affects and opens up dream work, so doing this at or near any full moon is best.

ITEMS NEEDED

Your bed

Salt

Your Fetch shrine

Your werewolf talisman

Some werewolf shape-shifting salve

A journal and pen by your bedside

THE EXERCISE

The first time you work with your Fetch in dream, you will just focus on meeting and playing with it to bond. After that, it is up to you. In the future, you'll be able to have your Fetch guide you in dream or take you to things you seek in dream.

To begin, sprinkle some salt around your bed as you do nine low up-growls to banish unwanted energies. Slowly turn around clockwise three times and up-howl once to the Moon Goddess, visualizing a ring of silver light surrounding and protecting your area. If you have installed your werewolf Fetch in a shrine, grab the shrine. If not, hold your talisman. Quietly up-howl "HA" three times to awaken and call your Fetch to you, visualizing its symbol and low growling its name. Put on your werewolf talisman.

Carefully rub a tiny bit of the werewolf salve on your third eye and on the back of your head. Turn off the light.

Lie in bed and silently call to your Fetch with its name and visualize its symbol until the image and symbol of the Fetch merge and are crystal clear. Tell your Fetch that you want to meet and play with it, hold it in your mind with love and excitement as you are falling asleep.

At this point, you may use the sexual energy of self-love in the liminal state between waking and sleeping while focusing on your Fetch and its symbol to intensify the link and the magick. Fall asleep focusing intently on your Fetch and its symbol while whispering its name.

Now, if at first you don't succeed, keep trying. If you are overtired, preoccupied by mundane thoughts, or just not in the mood, wait until you are more focused. Also, try it at different lunar phases. You may have more success at a new moon than a full moon. Experiment and persevere! With will and focus, you will succeed! Have fun in dreamland!

When you awaken and you have succeeded, immediately write down your dreams. Thank the Fetch, place the talisman on your side table or on the Fetch shrine, and take a shower with some of the salt. To finish the exercise, sweep up the salt on your floor, going counterclockwise, with three low down-growls. Wash the salt away as you like.

Once you have met and bonded with your werewolf Fetch in a dream, the intensity of this bond will grow and it can guide you in various dream realms or carry you to astral places you wish to explore. Try focusing on a symbol or a tarot card and asking your Fetch to take you into that realm. When dreaming, your Fetch may be able to converse with you as well. Listen carefully! Remember, your Fetch is a part of you, a helper and friend, not a servant.

Other Possible Fetch Work

At this point in your practice, your Fetch it is now a real entity bound to you as well as being a part of you. You should feel a deep personal resonance with your Fetch. This is the stage where it has become your personal Wolf Spirit helper, a guardian and helper as it were. Your Fetch has appeared to your inner eye often, but at this stage you (and others) may begin to see its form out of the corner of your eye or in shadows when it is out and about. At other times, its presence may be made known by the sound of paws, scratching, or even whispered barks and growls. At this point it will communicate with you at will and easily; you're best buds.

Your Fetch will also have evolved a personality, style, and maybe even communicated a gender of its own that reflects your Animalself. Your bond has been solidified and is now becoming more conscious. Even though it was and is a part of you, it has evolved a lot.

If you continue this practice, your werewolf Fetch will be a friend and possibly more useful. Your Fetch will function as a bridge between your deep unconscious mind and your often limited conscious mind in many ways. It will begin to "show" you magickal spells, sigils, runes, mediations, and so on from hidden places in meditation and dreams, if you ask. In many ways, this is how this book came into being: with the ongoing help of my Fetch, the Three-Eyed-Werewolf (no, not his secret name). Soon you will be able to conjure and invoke your own Fetch whenever necessary because of your bond.

Your Fetch will be able to hover near you to do your bidding by "riding in" your werewolf talisman as it did before. In this way it could actively guard you, act as an astral messenger, carry out spells, and so on. At this point, I assume you have plenty of ideas of how to keep your Fetch busy. Just remember, your Fetch is a partner and friend and needs constant feeding to maintain its independent form.

Astral Fetch Work and Riding the Fetch

A powerful use of your Fetch is to "ride" it. There are two ways this is traditionally done.

One way would be to astrally ride upon it, like riding a horse. In this case, a Fetch would appear as a werewolf or wolf and your spirit form rides it like a horse on whatever astral journeys you wish to do. There are many old medieval images of witches riding to the sabbat on the back of wolves or werewolves, which were probably Fetches or Familiars.

Another way to "ride" a Fetch would be to "wear" it. This means you'd let your Fetch's astral form settle upon you and over you like a full-body fur cloak. In this way your Fetch can "carry you" to various astral places or events, all while you are in deep trance or liminal state. This "wearing the skin" of your Fetch can also protect you when you are walking in a sketchy place or dancing and prowling in deep wilderness. Most animals, after all, fear and avoid wolves. Any werewolf magick rituals, spells, or practices you do will be more intense and potent if they are enhanced with the blended aura of a werewolf Fetch.

Letting the Fetch Rest

Whenever you are done working with your Fetch, in whatever manner, it is wise to "put it to bed" in its shrine or in the werewolf talisman and release it back to sleep to recoup. When doing so, treat it kindly like a good pup. Praise it, thank it, calm it down, and feed it.

CHAPTER 7

WEREWOLF RITUALS

———————— ╫ ————————

We have now mastered the key aspects of werewolf magick history, theory, and practices, including shape-shifting and Fetch work. With these skills, we can begin creating our own werewolf path. There is so much more that can be done with werewolf magick and so much lore and information still out there.

What follows are a number of eclectic rituals that exemplify the variety of possible werewolf magick practices. They are all creatively based on bits of lore and legends and some are revived older practices crafted into new rituals with ancient roots. All of them have been created by me in tandem with my Animalself in a personal creative fashion, using inspired ritual work involving shape-shifting and werewolf trances. I hope these rituals inspire you to create your own werewolf magick rituals, spells, and practices with the guidance you are now attuned to from your Animalself. Every shape-shifting opens your deep unconscious mind, unites you further with your Animalself and unleashes your magick and creativity. If you have done the work, you are now a full-on werewolf, a member of the werewolf magick pack! Many howls and success to your ongoing creative ritual work.

Hekate Lunar Wolf Spirit Ritual

The purpose of this invocation is to invoke the Goddess Hekate, Lady of the Crossroads, of magick, the moon, and protection. She is often represented by three wolves or as having three wolf heads. "Therefore we start seeing ideas manifest of wolves in company with Artemis and Hekate ... with very specific epithets that refer to wolves ..." [53]

She is the gateway to the deep unconscious mind and mother of the Animalself, often called upon by werewolf cults on dark moons. This invocation can be done for lycanthropic dream work, to empower your wolf-spirit or Fetch or to invoke spiritual power. It can also be used for protection for either yourself, women and children, or anyone in need. This ritual is inspired by passages from the Greek Magical Papyri [54]

SETUP

This ritual should be done near or on the new moon. It's more powerful if done at a crosspaths in the woods, but it can be anywhere wild or natural, even in a backyard. It is best to practice this ritual at night but it can be done in daylight as well. The main point is to avoid being disturbed. It would be best to do a bit of research on Hekate and get to know her before the ritual.

ITEMS NEEDED

Wear your werewolf talisman

A wooden or ceramic plate

A small cup of deep red wine

An image of Hekate

A twig of dried rosemary

A small black candle

Your ritual knife

Olive oil

Some honeycomb (or honey)

Red flowers

A few dried beans

---

53. Beloved in Light: Following the Path of Apollon, "Of Dogs and Wolves."

54. Betz, *The Greek Magical Papyri in Translation*, PGM IV. 2714–34, PGM IV. 2708–84, PGM IV. 2441–2621.

The Ritual

Bring your things to the crosspaths. Place all the items on the simple wooden or ceramic plate at the center of the intersecting paths. Pause and collect yourself. Feel the woods at night, silently honor the Lord of the Forest, Gaia, and the Moon Goddess. Up-howl softly to honor this place and the spirits here. Think deeply about your purpose, whatever it is and then begin the Praxis Shifting Rite. Up-growl three times while powerfully throwing open your arms and paws while turning counterclockwise. Concentrate on banishing any interfering spirits or energies. Then, turning clockwise, sprinkle wine around you in a circle and pour a few drops upon the platter/altar, proclaiming three times:

Io Evoe Hekate!

Hold up the plate toward the dark moon, offering the items to Hekate while low up-howling three times. Pause and feel the darkness swirl about you until the image of Hekate forms in your mind's eye. Bow to her and be aware of yourself as a werewolf honoring a wolf goddess.

Up-growl three times while lighting the candle and with all your will silently call to Hekate while focusing on your desire. Then, in a growly voice invoke her with these words:

Hekate, you of three faces,
Come to me for I love you!
With loving attention, hearken to this sacred call:
You are of night the youthful, dawn-lit bringer of vibrant lunar light
You who rides upon a bull with fiery eyes!
O Queen of shadows,
You drive your chariot alongside that of the Sun God
You dance in triple wolf-forms as three Goddesses
You dance with the stars.
You are Justice and the Wyrd of the Fates!
O Three Headed One
You transform into all forms

You illuminate as a glowing lamp in darkness,
You roar like a bull and laugh like a stream
O night howler who loves solitude
Oh Mother of Wolves
Open all wild hearts!
You howl with the voice of wolves
You wear three wolf heads!
Your paws are of a wolf,
All wolves and savage dogs adore you!
I call you to me, one of many names
You appear as Artemis who shines at night and hunts deer
You also howl with three voices!
As three Headed Selene!
O Trident Bearing One of three Paths
You offer me three paths and hold three undying flames
You embody three ways O Mistress of the Three Times
Help me as I invoke you and grant my request
Free my werewolf self that I may do my will!
You embody the vast world at night,
You make the dark spirits shudder and the gods tremble!
O many named Goddess who manifests the power of Nature, O Great Mother!
You bring forth both Gods and men for You all things come,
and by you all things end O Eternal One.
Io Evoe Hekate! Io Evoe Hekate! Io Evoe Hekate!

Now, light the dried rosemary and leave it on the plate, smoldering. Raise
your paws up and growl:

I offer you sweet smoke, O ancient Hekate!
Arrow Shooter, heavenly one, you Goddess of deep dark waters
You who run up mountains, Goddess of crossroads!
Night one who guards the underworld as a three headed wolf,
You are the Wildness of night, darkness, and chaos,

You are Fate, Wyrd, One who kills and also brings justice
You control Cerberus for you are Cerberus!
You are feast on hearts and flesh
You whose howls echoes about the graves
You who incite wanderings of the wild wolf madness,
Come now to my ritual and help me!
Io Hekate
Io Hekate
Io Evoe Hekate!

Crouch over the plate, candle, and incense and down-growl nine times as you feel her power envelop and bless you. Put a finger to your lips and silence your voice and mind. See her form slowly appear in your mind's eye as a black she-wolf, as a three-wolf-headed woman or in another form she offers to you alone. Focus on your wolfish desire.

Prick your paw with the knife and let three drops of blood fall onto the plate. Hekate will then show you a secret symbol or image concerning your request or whisper into your ear. Your hackles may rise and you may feel a chill, this is a good sign. Sit in silence and be with her.

When the communion and magick feels like it is winding down, honor Hekate with three low up-howls. Taste then offer all the items on the plate to Hekate. Drink and pour out the last of the wine to her. Now, blow out the candle and take up the plate, candle, and the knife. Make sure nothing is still lit. Then leave all the offerings on the ground at the crossroads for the wild kin.

Stand, paws raised, and up-howl one last time in thanks to all. Then turn counterclockwise clapping and up-growling to the three directions used earlier and see all excess energy fly away.

Sway and stomp your paws on the earth and down-growl "MA" rhythmically several times. Let the trance state fade as you return to human form and mind. Finish by placing your hands on the earth, down-growling three times to let Gaia take any excess energies. Feel the spell settle in your bones. Stand, howl, then go. Embrace the now welcoming dark woods and stalk your way home. Write down your results. Keep the image of Hekate by your bed and await the dreams and transformations inspired by her.

Solar Werewolf Empowerment Ritual

Though the werewolf gnosis is often associated with the night and the moon, there are a number of ancient solar wolf deities and werewolf cults as we have seen. The following empowerment ritual can be performed anytime when you need to energize the body, mind, or aura; protect yourself or others from danger; or just fill yourself with "uplifting solar spirit." Much of werewolf magick focuses on shifting, a process which is in large part powered by the fire chakra or solar plexus (located above the belly button). All werewolf magick work requires a vast amount of fiery energy and this spell can help replenish it if you're feeling low. All of the gods invoked here are wolf-associated sun gods and they shine a protective and blessing light of werewolf magick.

Setup

This ritual should be practiced on a clear sunny day, beginning early in the morning, ideally sunrise. Do this anywhere you like as long as you can see the sun and have a bit of privacy. This ritual has four different sections that are to be done over a day at dawn, midday, sunset, and midnight, so make sure to set aside a day to be able to do all four parts. The four invocations that follow should be done facing the following directions: dawn facing east, midday facing south, sunset facing west, and midnight facing north.

Before you start, visualize a flaming golden solar wolf shining in the sun, filled with power and light within the solar orb sending rays of blessing to you. It's recommended to do the Praxis Shifting Rite before each invocation during the day to really empower the ritual.

When doing each of the four invocations, both of your paws should be raised up to the direction of the sun during the invocations to visualize the golden solar wolf. As you finish the invocations, cross your arms over your chest and absorb the power.

If this ritual is being done for a specific protection, a germane item may be held. The energy from this ritual may also be directed to a specific body part in need of healing. If it is being done for future protection work, a small golden candle inscribed with an appropriate glyph can be used. Such a candle can be blessed with this ritual and given to another to provide protection as well.

ITEMS NEEDED
Yourself and your imagination
Clean clothes

THE RITUAL
The ritual is complete when each of the invocations has been done over the course of one day.

Dawn invocation:
Apollo Lycaeus!
Great Wolf power!
You come as a wolf of light
Leaping forth in glory
To chase away the night and fear!
Sun wolf!
Come to me!
Give protection and power!
May I shine as a wolf!

Midday invocation:
Lupercus!
Golden Sun Wolf!
You fill the heavens with sparkling glory
Center of all triumphing joy
You banish all doubts and pain!
Sun wolf!
Come to me!
Give protection and power!
May I shine as a wolf!

Sunset invocation:
Apollo Cunomaglos
Wolf Lord Hunter!
Golden predator of evil
Carry the sun into the darkness
Bringing me light and strength!
Sun wolf!
Come to me!
Give protection and power!
May I shine as a wolf!

Midnight invocation:
Soranus Apollo!
Shining lord of volcanic fires
Fill me with the inner power
Protector and guide of the Dead
Dispel darkness with your dance of fire[55]
Sun wolf!
Come to me!
Give protection and power!
May I shine as a wolf!

The Divine Wolf Star Ritual

The Wolf Star, also known as the Dog Star, is a famous and powerful star known to us as Sirius and Sothis to the Greeks. Other cultures like the ancient Chinese and Pawnee Native Americans named the star the "Wolf Star." Invoking this guiding star of werewolf magick centers wers and guides them to help them remain focused and balanced. This invocation is about equilibrium, empowering, and protecting any werewolf magick. This is a good ritual to practice if you feel a bit unbalanced while invoking the wolf-power.

---

55. Referencing werewolf cult priests of Soranus, the Hirpini Sorani, who danced on burning coals.

SETUP

Practice this ritual on a very clear night when you know Sirius will be in the sky. One way to find Sirius is to first find Orion in the sky and follow the stars that make up his belt down to the brightest star, which is Sirius. This can be done alone, or with your pack if you share werewolf magick with others. As with most werewolf magick, it should be done in wilderness as much as possible. However, it can be done anywhere with a view of the star and where you won't be bothered at night. Simply doing the invocation when wolfing around at night and catching sight of Sirius can be powerful, but it is better to do the full ritual. You will need to have a copy of the Sirius sigil and a way to draw it so you can stand on it.

Figure 12: The Sirius Sigil

ITEMS NEEDED

A place with cleared earth or sand under your feet to draw the sigil or materials to draw it on a large piece of paper and pen

A werewolf magick wand or stang

Sprigs of both fresh and dried juniper.

A small plate or shell to burn the dried juniper on

A glass of red wine

A beryl crystal (blue is best) if you want to create a wolf star talisman to use in the future

THE RITUAL

Assemble the items near you and center yourself. Turning clockwise, up-growl three times waving the stang to banish any unwanted energies. With the wand or stang, carefully draw the Sirius sigil on the earth or sand. Up-howl three times to call to the wolf star. If you are drawing the sigil on a large piece of paper, do so with a pen or marker and when finished, charge the image by touching it with the end of the stang and up-howling three times to call to the wolf star. The sigil, an ancient symbol of Sirius, should be large enough so you can stand upon it. As you do so, raise your paws, face the star, and say:

Sothis, Sirius, Wolfstar! I call to thee
Glowing atop the great world tree
By this star-sign and holy mark
I invoke your magick ray, illuminate the dark!
Sothis Asteri!
Io Evoe!

When done, up-howl three times. Touch the stang or wand to the sigil. See the glyph glowing an intense almost neon blue. Place the cup of red wine or juice in the center of the diamond part of the sigil, the wolf eye. Place the fresh juniper sprig into the wine. Light the dried juniper and walk around the sigil clockwise saying:

Wolf ray, wolf light
Wolf power, wolf might
Spirit true, spirit sight
Guide this wolf
Burning bright!
Balanced, centered
So may I be
Wolf with man
Sothis Asteri!

Leave the smoldering juniper in the bowl at the top of the sigil. Raise both paws high and focus on the star. Do the Praxis Shifting Rite to go into a trance state as a wer; the star will shine much brighter and you'll feel it in this trance state.

Now, see the forces of the star beaming down, filling your sigil and your body as you call the energy down from this star. Slowly down-howl a long heartfelt invocation and see the beam of power filling your circle with a calming and balancing light as you growl the following:

Hail unto you who are Sothis always shining,
Even unto you who are sun beyond sun,
Eternal Wolf Star, you never set or rise,
But emerge as the Sacred Wolf Guide from darkness
Praise unto you, O Wolf whose body is of star fire
Hail to the blazing star beaming from your third eye
Piercing, centering, calming my Animalself with love
You are the divine emanation behind all the wer
The star goddess stands in her glory about you
And the feral child of silence is your heart's center.
Hail unto you from the abodes of the eternal,
Hail!

Down-howl three times as fully as possible and then inhale the powerful blessing ray from the star with a "HA" sound. Feel it enter the top of your head, descend, open your third eye, flow down your spinal column illuminating your heart and your loins, and then ground down into the sigil. Now glowing, pick up the cup of wine and hold it, seeing all this glowing power condensing and centering into a shining incandescent star within the cup. Take a sip. Place your finger to your lips and close your eyes as the light coalesces and glows brightly from your heart center. Now the power of the wolf star fills your being, centering and balancing you.

When done, pour out the rest of the wine onto the sigil but place a drop on your heart and the beryl, if you have one. Give final thanks to the lovely wolf star Sirius with a long, low up-howl. Ground yourself, by stomping, swaying, and down-growling "MA" until your werewolf form has faded. Leave by walking out in a counterclockwise spiral from the center, shuffling and erasing the sigil.

(If you drew it on paper, tear it with your feet and recycle it.) See the excess energies flowing into the earth. Touch the earth, thank Gaia, and then go.

Lupus Dei Ritual to Defeat Evil Sorcerers or Entities

Medieval witchcraft trial documents that recorded the confessions of those accused of lycanthropy sometimes referenced werewolves who insisted that they were "good" werewolf cult members who fought evil spirits, demons, or "witches" on the astral plane to protect humans. This is where the term "lupus dei," which means "wolf of god" or "dog of god," comes from. They spoke in detail about how they would slip into a trance, become werewolves and defend humans on what we call the astral plane. Once a year they would all shape-shift and fly into hell and defeat evil devil-loving sorcerers to protect their country and humans. It does seem logical that spirit and real wolves would be excellent defenders. This simple ritual is based on these ancient testimonies. To be successful with this ritual you need to be fairly proficient with shape-shifting, trance work, and Fetch work as laid out in the previous chapters.

Setup

This operation can be done anytime and anywhere a friend, a pack member, or you are being psychically attacked by a nasty person or spirit entity. This ritual also works well for driving out malicious ghosts or poltergeists from a haunted space. You'll need to prepare a quiet and protected place where you can enter a trance state safely. It can be done in a chair, in your own bed, on a comfortable recliner, or even outside in the woods in a warm sleeping bag. Your head should point north if possible. The room and area should be clean. Dress in clean, comfortable, loose clothes, red if possible. You should also wear your werewolf magick talisman and any other protective amulets you have.

Items Needed

Loose comfortable clothes

Some salt

Red pepper flakes

A small plate

Three glasses of pure water, one with lemon for drinking

A red candle

A small physical "link" item from the place or person being attacked

Your ritual knife used for werewolf magick

Your werewolf talisman

Some dark chocolate

THE RITUAL

Begin by taking a ritual bath or shower with some of the salt sprinkled on you or in the water. As you do so growl:

Out tout
Throughout and about
All good come in
All evil stay out

Set up a small altar next to your bed or chair. Place the red pepper flakes in the small plate and put the red candle on top of them. Put the cups of water on either side of the candle and place the "link" item in front of the candle. Think about the person or place that is under psychic attack. Get mad. Repeat the same chant in a growly voice and sprinkle salt in a clockwise circle about your entire sleeping area:

Out tout
Throughout and about
All good come in
All evil stay out

Deeply and intensely up-growl three times as you get ready for an astral smackdown! Do the Praxis Shifting Rite, then light the candle and face it. Continue up-growling and swaying; get pumped up and martial. Take a few pepper flakes from the plate and chew them. In a riled up growly voice, spit out this invocation:

As Wolf of God this is my will
To honor, Wildness, Wyrd and Way
Protect from harm and always kill
All harmful spirits, come what may.
Wolfish gods hunt with me
As I set my spirit free
Lupus Dei, so mote it be!
FIAT!

Up-howl a martial "Bring it!" howl. Light the candle and hold the dagger. Up-growl three times and trace a circle of glowing red protection about you clockwise. Keep up-growling! Now, place the dagger and the link item under your pillow.

Put on your werewolf talisman and any other protective amulets. Return to swaying but now switch to rhythmic down-growling as you work your way deeper and deeper into a werewolf trance state … when you are in full liminal state, lie or sit down.

Breathe deeply, keep down-growling, blur your vision and go deeper into the trance state. Feel your Animalself wolf getting restless, feel your body getting loose and free. Close your eyes and sink into the trance state, still down-growling but quieter and deeper.

Call to your Fetch and summon it from your werewolf talisman or shrine by visualizing its symbol glowing red on your third eye. When the Fetch appears, silently tell it that you are going to ride it into battle by entering it so it will carry your consciousness. Your Fetch will be excited. Focus on your Fetch; whether you see your Fetch as a wolf or werewolf doesn't matter. Stare into its eyes. It must be absolutely clear and in focus.

Now, as you focus on the eyes of your Fetch, slowly move its symbol from your third eye to its third eye and as you do so, move some of your consciousness into it. See yourself becoming more transparent as the now-glowing form of your Fetch becomes clearer, more vibrant, and now glowing red. Touch the dagger and the link item as you fully sink into the Fetch and the astral. Know that it will guard your body.

You know your quiet human form is lying there and protected, but your consciousness is now in the form of your Fetch. Your Fetch and you have expanded into a huge, terrifying beast with sharp claws and teeth and a primal will to hunt and kill all evil. When ready, open your third eye / spirit vision and will yourself to fly to the person, place, or area under attack. If you're not sure of the precise location, focus on the danger, touch the link item, and follow where the glowing energy sends you.

Once you are there and have seen the malefic hostile astral entity, attack the entity with a terrifying howl. Give no quarter. Hunt your prey; chase it as a wolf chases a rabbit. Pounce, bite, tear, and destroy it. If the entity is more powerful, fight like crazy and injure it until it flees and then bid your astral werewolf Fetch to return to your human body. If the nasty follows you, fly back to your body, take up the dagger, and stab the evil astral entity in the heart. You will be protected by the salt circle and the dagger, being charged, will kill it or send it fleeing. Often simply showing up on the astral as a terrifying wolf will send malignant entities fleeing, including lost ghosts, wimpy sorcerers, minor demons, or ghouls and such.

When the battle is done and you have kicked astral ass, howl on the astral plane and pound your astral wolfy chest! Will your Fetch to rejoin your spirit to your body. Call your consciousness to separate from the Fetch and drift back down into your physical entranced body as the excited Fetch hovers above you. Silently communicate with your Fetch, sincerely thank and praise it, and promise to feed it later. Snuggle your conscious back into your body and begin to breathe deeply while rumble growling. Reintegrate slowly and shift to low rhythmic down-growling as you release the Fetch to slowly fall back into your werewolf talisman or shine, curl up, and fall asleep. Slowly sit up, drink the lemon water and eat the chocolate. Then place a bit of salt under your tongue. When ready to rise, do so and say:

As darkness dispelled by rising sun
By wolfen gods and moon mother three

I sheath my claws, fangs and sword
May peace now reign, so mote it be!

Blow out the candle. Scatter some of the pepper flakes counterclockwise about the room with three banishing up-growls. Sheath the dagger. Gather much of the salt and take a bath or shower with it. It is done. Hail the conquering astral werewolf lupus dei!

CHAPTER 8

WEREWOLF MAGICK WITH THE DEAD

―――――――――― ‖‖ ――――――――

L et's face it, to most—maybe not you, dear reader—werewolves are scary and are often grouped up with other scary beings like vampires, ghosts, and demons. Werewolves, as you have seen, were connected with cults that often were about battle, war, protection, and ferocity, all things wolves are known for. Along with the ferocity and warrior connections comes, of course, death and wolves have long been associated with death. There has always been a connection between the shadowy realm that connects the living and the dead with shape-shifting and particularly with werewolfery. Early neolithic hominid graves have been discovered that contained wolf bones and teeth in ceremonial arrangements.[56] Wolves and werewolf magick have had a close relationship with death and the underworld because they share the reality of liminal states. Werewolf gods and goddesses often show this aspect. Odin is known, among other things, as a god of death and his Valkyrie women warrior spirits gathered up the heroic dead while flying on the backs of wolves. Wolfish goddesses like Hekate, who is connected to the underworld with Hades, has been connected with spirits of the dead.

Also, many festivals and rituals where werewolves play a part are held at times of the year when the veil between life and what lies beyond is thinnest, Halloween or the Samhain as examples.[57]

―――――――――――――――――――――

56. Losey, "Canids As Persons: Early Neolithic Dog and Wolf Burials, Cis-Baikal, Siberia."
57. Jackson, *The Compleat Vampyre: The Vampyre Shaman, Werewolves, Witchery & the Dark Mythology of the Undead*, 30–34.

So here, in this shadowy liminal chapter, we have gathered all the werewolf rites and spells from many types of folklore connected with conversing with or honoring the dead. May the spirit of the wolf always guide, protect, and offer solace to those who have passed on.

Werewolf Spell to Learn of the Past or Future from the Dead

The purpose of this spell is to talk to the dead to gain information. It is based on Icelandic sorcery where the shape-shifting Vitki, or shaman, would access "straight paths" or ley lines upon which the dead traveled. The Raido "R" rune used in this spell represents a horse, traveling, and also death and communication with the dead.

Setup

This spell was traditionally done on Midsummer night, the summer solstice, but it can be done during any "liminal" time, my favorite choice being Samhain. It should be done at midnight.

Before it gets too dark find a crosspaths; at least one of the roads or paths should lead to a graveyard, but improvise if needed. Prepare an ax or hatchet ahead of time with the Blessing Ritual in chapter 3 and paint two eyes with the Raido rune on it. Think about what you want the dead to tell you. Know and be able to visualize the Raido rune:

Figure 13: Raido Rune

Items Needed

A canid fur wrap or belt, a black ritual cloak

Your werewolf talisman

A dried sprig or yew and a small shell or bowl for burning it in

A hatchet or ax that has been spiritually cleansed and charged

An offering to the dead spirits of pure tobacco

Three silver coins (dimes are fine)

THE SPELL

At midnight, bring the items to the empty crosspaths. Bow to each direction and do a low up-growl. Face down the road or path that leads to the graveyard. Focus on what you want the dead to tell you. Put on the fur cloak or belt and werewolf talisman. Do the Praxis Shifting Rite. Light the dried yew in the bowl and spin clockwise three times, growling with a deep "RRRR" sound, then end facing the graveyard direction. Place the smoking herb on the path and call on the mighty dead to aid you with a low moaning up-howl. Take up the ax and stand in the center of the crossroads.

Hold the ax by the handle, blade facing out, to each of the four directions as you turn clockwise. Face the blade up to the heavens and finally strike the blade into the earth (and the underworld) growling "Rrrrr rrrrr rrrrr." Then do a low and mournful whine. Leave the ax stuck in the path, visualize a cleft opening where it is embedded, and "see" it open to the underworld. Sway and up-growl more as you visualize the unseen astral forces arise and swirl about you.

Take up the ax or hatchet and clean the dirt off the blade. The gate is now open. Squat before the "cleft." Hold the ax up to your liminal vision with the sharp edge facing you. Focus on the edge, breathe deeply, and let the trance pull you into that edge it until slowly expands and fills all your astral sight and the edge becomes a road to the other world that the dead walk. Slowly and deeply growl the following:

raidho raidho raidho

r r r r r r r r r

ru ra ri re ro

r r r r r r r r r

When you're finished, you'll be able to feel the spirits of the dead awaken. Project your wer consciousness along the edge of the blade, which has become your astral path. As you do so, silently call for the dead to meet you to give you knowledge of the past or the future. Soon you will see the spirits of the dead coming toward you upon that path. When they approach, silently honor and bless them, and ask what you want to know. They will communicate with you if they want but it's not always guaranteed. If they choose not to, sever the connection and go as per the end of this spell. If they agree, commune with them. Sprinkle the offering of tobacco. Take great note of the visions and information they tell or show you.

When you are done, bid them goodbye. If they try to follow you, up-growl intently and bid them goodbye. They will go. In this astral form "walk" backward and pull away from the path until you are looking at the blade again. Come back to your body and place the ax down and earth yourself by stomping, swaying, and down-growling "MA" until you are wer no longer.

Bury the three coins in the crossroads in the cleft your ax made as a thanks and payment; low down-howl your thanks and blessing. Light the dry yew in the bowl; circle three times counterclockwise so the smoke can dismiss all spirits and cleanse you. Take up the ax and use the shaft to pound the ground three times to "seal" the cleft to the underworld. Go forth with what you learned.

Rite to Travel a "Deadway"
and Meet with a Shade of the Dead

This is a rite to find, activate, and travel along astral "deathways" to meet with a spirit, help a spirit, or to simply visit with them. Some traditions describe hidden pathways where the dead and werewolves travel in spirit form. The author Montague Summers mentions that many ancient pre-Celtic cromlechs and caverns mark these "spirit or werewolf paths" and called them "deadways." In Germany these same spirit or werewolf paths were referred to as "Woton's Pathways."[58]

SETUP

This rite assumes a certain amount of practice and skill with Fetch work as described in chapter 6. It is best done at liminal times of the year, like near

---

58. Jackson, *The Compleat Vampyre: The Vampyre Shaman, Werewolves, Witchery & the Dark Mythology of the Undead,* 95.

Samhain, just before Yule, or any dark moon. Some research will be needed to find ancient burial areas, graves, or haunted areas where you can find some of the "hidden paths" that flow from our world to the spirit world. Once you find one, visit it, maybe choose a stone from it, and use this in your work at home to direct you. Set your goal for the working before starting the rite. You will be "riding" your Fetch form to the realm of the dead to meet with a loved one who has passed on. Be clear on the intention.

If you are brave or adventurous, this can be done while camping out right on a "deadway" or spirit-line. However, it's fine and safer to do it at home, on a couch or on a carpeted floor with a mat, *but not in your bed*. Start this rite at sunset.

ITEMS NEEDED

Loose clothing

A small black cloth for an altar

A werewolf magick stang or a new stang made for necromantic werewolfery
  from willow

Dark wine or liquor

Two small twigs of juniper, one dried, one fresh

A small bowl to burn the dried juniper in

Four twigs from a rowan or mountain ash tree

One bay leaf

Your ritual knife

A black candle and holder

If done outside: a sleeping bag and camping gear

If done inside: a stone or other token from the deadway you found or a clear
  idea where it is

Your werewolf talisman

A small onyx for protection

Pure water to drink

Healthy snack food like nuts, dried fruit, or apples

THE RITE

Begin at sunset and lay the black altar cloth on the floor or earth facing north or in the direction of the "deadway" you will follow. Next, assemble your items on the altar cloth with the stang lying before it or propped up behind it. Fill the cup with wine. Then, light the dried juniper in the bowl and carry it counter-clockwise about your ritual space while up-growling nine times. Next, do the Praxis Shifting Rite.

As you growl and rock, go deeper into trance than usual; activate your werewolf senses and second sight until you can sense the unseen. Then, pick up the stang, hold it by the "horns," and align it to the direction of the dead-way you wish to travel. Much of this work is intuitive and being in a deep werewolf state of consciousness and prowling about with your stang will help you feel this sacred pathway. Once you have found the deadway you should "see" the glowing path. Place the stang on the ground so that it is pointing in that direction.

Take up the rowan twigs, circle clockwise about your area with them, low up-howling three times and see a ring of protective silver energy form around your work area. Place the rowen twigs about your circle, one at each of the cardinal directions. Your body will now be safe and no harm shall come to it.

Take the bay leaf and with the tip of the knife, write the name of the spirit you wish to visit the leaf. Prick your finger and put blood on it. Keep the blood-marked bay leaf on your heart during the rite.

Sprinkle a bit of wine in the direction of the deadway you will travel while "riding" your Fetch. Low up-howl three times to honor this time and place and the dead. Rock and up-growl or use other werewolf lingo that feels right to deepen your werewolf shift-trance until you can see the shadowy silver thread of the line of the deadway you will travel.

Growl your purpose and the deceased person's name. Low up-howl to them; feel them awaken to your distant howl. They know you are coming. Sway, shape-shift deeper, and prowl one more time clockwise about your area; grow, and bark in a more excited rising voice, call to the spirit of the dead! Light the candle on the altar and growl the following invocation:

Werewolf Lord Of Wildness
Lord of the Dead
Lord of the Forest
Of hallows, of dread
Open this gate
Your werewolf am I
By the Wyrd and the Way
May my Fetch fly
Along your dark path
Through cleft of shade
Protect my flesh
In this sacred glade
Open the mystery
Below and above
That I may commune
With one whom I love
Nox fiat!

Slide into your sleeping bag or your bedding on the floor, making sure you are warm and snug. Keep the bay leaf on your heart and cross your arms over it. Up-howl a long, low, dirge-like howl as you feel and catch a glimmer of the dead soul you seek.

The Fetch Work

Slow your breath and continue the long deep growling until it is just rumbling as you shift deeper and enter the trance. Using your will, call your werewolf Fetch to you through your talisman. When you can clearly see your Fetch, slip into it like a robe and look through its eyes at the now luminous silver path. Push, leap, and fly while riding your Fetch. Soon you are flowing and running down the silver deadway path. As you race down it all about you except the glowing path is a blur that soon becomes darker and darker …

Suddenly you enter a very dim grotto with no sign of the sky amongst monstrous trees. The path slopes down but the silver thread is luminous and you flow along it with confidence and power and no fear, for you ride within a mighty wolf-beast. You encounter many phantoms and entities and some may be frightening. If you ever feel fear, show your fangs and growl and all will be well, for you are sacred here in the land of the dead and you bear upon your chest a glowing bay leaf, your passport. You reach the heart of the grotto full of the largest trees and come to a place that is clearly sacred with a large stone. Upon the stone will be standing the ghost of the one you seek. If he or she is pleased to see you, touch the glowing bay leaf at your heart. If they smile, they are who they seem. If not, you will know.

The rest I cannot say and even what has been written here may not be what you witness, for it is your astral journey. May you have a powerful and loving visit.

When you feel a deep tug from your body, it is time to go. Offer the essence of the wine to the one you have visited, bless them, and offer to help them and listen to the reply. Then receive their blessing and the wisdom or knowledge you sought.

Bid your Fetch to return and race back along the silver path through many amazing places and the blurred surroundings will lighten until you land back in your flesh with a werewolf leap and a physical jolt. Lie still and adjust. Thank your Fetch and dismiss it. Do not forget to feed it later! It has done well.

Inhale and exhale slowly and deeply, then down-growl "MA" with every exhaled breath and feel your astral consciousness and physical bodies reintegrate. Be still, let your body earth itself. Lie there and strive to recall the encounter and hold fast to the memories. Write them down as soon as you can.

To end, stand up and light the dried juniper in the bowl again. Carry it counterclockwise about your ritual space while up-growling nine times to banish all spirits and entities. Collect the rowen twigs and put them on the altar. Now, burn the bay leaf you've had at your heart in the burning bowl. Growl:

Bones and ashes deep in Earth
All that dies will have rebirth
Darkest shadow to brightest light
In werewolf eyes, burning bright

By sister moon and mother tree
The dead are loved and I am free!

Blow out the candle, drain the cup of wine, and up-howl three times with a feeling of renewal! Savor the life you have, honor the dead you love, and give thanks to your Fetch, your Animalself, and the gods of nature who give all things.

Ritual for Honoring and Guiding the Dead with Anpu

This ritual is a bit of an outlier because it honors and invokes an ancient Egyptian werewolf god, Anubis or Anpu, a deity not mentioned until now because until the writing of this book I did not know there was actually a wolf god. Calling upon Anubis, I was given this ritual and so offer it here.

The goal of this ritual is to take on the werewolf aspect of Anpu to aid and help guide a loved one who has died or to aid the dead in whatever way is needed. Working with ancestors is powerful magick and has always been part of werewolf magick. Anpu is one of the most powerful and well-known Egyptian gods, but did you know that the "jackal" form of Anpu was actually a "golden wolf" according to new genetic research?[59] This may also explain why Anpu was called golden though always depicted as black in imitation of the bodies of the dead. It is this golden werewolf god who traditionally prepares and guides the dead as they move through the underworld, Amenta. Anpu also guides the barque of the sun god Ra as it traverses the underworld. Anpu is often connected with another underworld wolfish god, Wepwawet, who was a different wolf species.

SETUP

There are multiple ways to use this ritual. It can be used soon after someone you love has passed if your goal is to help with their transition through death. If working with someone who has been deceased a long time, any liminal time of the year where the barrier between the living and the dead is thin is appropriate. Samhain, Yule, and dark moons are all appropriate times, but also do it when it feels right for you.

---

59. Hance, "Egyptian Jackal is Actually Ancient Wolf."

Set up a small altar facing west, the direction of the Egyptian afterlife, with the items noted below. Study images of Anpu so you can clearly visualize his black wolfish head and form.

ITEMS NEEDED

Frankincense incense and a small plate or bowl to burn it on

A black candle

A cup of very dark beer

An appropriate sacred cup for the beer

A small picture and/or item of the one who has died

An image of Anpu

An ankh (seen below) made of any material; homemade is fine (To bless it, see
the blessing ritual at the end of chapter 3.)

Figure 14: Ankh

THE RITUAL

Light some incense. Then, counterclockwise, lunge and project protection-power in the four cardinal directions, each time growling:

Begone evil!

Do the Praxis Shifting Rite and as you shift, picture yourself becoming an Anpu-like werewolf. Center yourself as this "Anpu-wer." Cross your hands over you chest.

Then, take the ankh by the loop and, clockwise, use it to make the sign of the ankh by tracing the ankh shape at each direction: loop, then crosspiece, then vertical line, howling each time as you "see" the ankh image glowing golden. Do this once more over your altar, up-growling three times:

Hail Anpu!

Light the candle. Make an offering by holding up the beer and bow to the god while saying:

I honor you, O Anpu,
Lord of the place of preparing the dead
You who are lord of the sacred land
You are foremost of those in the west
You are he who is upon the mountains
You are he who guides the dead,
Who protects the souls of the dead,
Who loves the dead, your children
Who brings the souls to new lives!
Be here now and let me see through your eyes
So that (name of deceased) *may be guided and protected*
And be healed of all afflictions and so be joyful in new life!
Hail Anpu!

Now, take time to rock and low up-growl to deepen your werewolf trance while shifting completely into the form of Anpu. Silently ask Anpu to come and empower you with his Ka, or Double. All becomes dark about you as Anpu gently covers you with this power as a cloak.

Hold your paws up, arms to the side and elbows bent in the gesture of the Ka. As your trance deepens and you become the Anpu-wer, you now "wear" the mask of Anpu and have become him. Down-growl three times and then growl:

I become Anpu!

Now focus on the image of the deceased person you wish to work with and use the ankh to draw an ankh shape around the picture or item. See it glowing gold. Close your eyes, raise your hands to shoulder height, and thrust both hands forward. Project your vision-consciousness through the loop of the glowing ankh image. You are entering the underworld where the shade of the person you wish to work with is waiting for you.

Envision yourself traveling as a priest of Anpu across desert sands empty of life to an oasis filled with trees and animals. In the center is a temple to Anpu, open to the sky and surrounded by greenery. Visualize it clearly, see the statue of Anpu within and bow to it. There, before it, waiting for you, is the shade of the one you seek. Now, you are with that person, but in Anpu-wer form. Telepathically connect with them and say:

I am (your real name) but I am now a priest of Anpu in order to travel here and see you. I am here to protect, guide, and offer help, love, and blessings to you.

What do you need of me? Do you have words for me?

Commune with the beloved dead one, listen, see, understand. There, in the underworld do what that soul asks of you. Comfort them. If they are not sure what they need, gently guide them through the jungle to the entrance of the halls of Amenta and then help them find the glowing golden door with an ankh upon it leading to new life and rebirth, if that is their will.

All of this will be deep and personal. Scenes will shift and change because all this is about you and the one who has died. If negative beings appear, remember you wear the power of the fearsome wolf-headed god Anpu, lord of the dead! With full godlike force, do the sign of the enterer at the creature and tell them to begone!

Work with your deceased loved one. Feel sorrow, love, joy as you will and need to. When this deep work is done, place your index finger to your lips and will your soul to return to the temple. Honor Anpu, and go.

Retrace your path as a priest of Anpu, pull your astral self back to your body by the light that links you to it. When you return to your body, breathe deep for several minutes. Place your index finger to your lips. Let the spirit and power of Anpu flow out of you as you quietly down-howl three times. Slowly rock and stomp your paws and down-howl "HA" quietly until all wer form has faded and you are again human. Take time for this process as you return to human form and consciousness.

With deep gratitude, burn a bit more frankincense and raise your hands up either side of you, as before, and say to the god:

Hail Anpu!
I thank you for your wisdom, teachings, aspect and blessing.
Thank you for guiding, protecting and helping me aid (deceased)
Most ancient wolf-god,
Bless and guide me through life and death, with love.
Life and love to Anpu!

Shake yourself. Hold up the chalice with the beer, offer it to Anpu, and drink the rest. Then say:

Wildness, Way, through Wyrd
Honor to the golden wolf who guides
The love we feel is ever heard
So their Ka into the Light glides!
Hail Anpu!

When you're done, stand and then lunge in the sign of the enterer and down-growl to each of the four directions, counterclockwise, banishing the whole area as you did before. After each lunge, simply visualize a golden wind blowing all energies away.

Then down-growl three times with your arms crossed over your chest and visualize a golden ankh glowing at your heart center that slowly dissolves while filling you with golden light. Say:

Begone evil!
Hail Maat!

Blow out the candle and go forth.

CHAPTER 9

WEREWOLF MAGICK SPELLS

———————— ||| ————————

Spells are like short rituals or rites that have a specific purpose or goal, such as bringing money, love, health, or protection. Spells accomplish things and are practical in the sense that they are like magickal tools or programs: there is always a desired specific end result other than general spiritual empowerment or experiences. The power, intensity, and astral focus of werewolf magick and werewolf Fetch work can be used in this way and likely has been over the ages. Once you have become accomplished at shape-shifting and channeling the immense power of your Animalself, why not use it in an ethical manner with spells? Wolves are more honorable than most humans: they only kill to eat and only fight to protect the pack and generally avoid aggression, always focusing on the prosperity of the pack. Cast spells like a wolf and you can't go wrong.

Invocation of Faunus Lycan

This is an invocation to be done in or at the edge of a dense forest on the full moon. It is for general blessing and to aid communion with the werewolf Lord of the Forest, Faunus Lycan.

Setup

The best place to do this spell would be a quiet forest, a wooded area, or wild place of your choosing. Try to do this spell on a day with a clear sky and full moon. Dress in loose clothing, green if possible.

Items Needed

No other items required, though you can have a glass of wine if you offer a bit
after.

The invocation

Faunus Lycan, I call to thee

By open moon and sacred tree

Rip the veil and open the gate

Star filled world

My thirst to slake

Fill with fury, power, desire

Fur of lightning eyes of fire

Make me Beast, I am thy plan

By horn and fang

And the great god Pan

Whip me with wolf skins

Cords bite and caress

Filled with ecstasy, so I am blessed

Break all bounds, shatter all chains,

Free me from fetters and all that restrains!

Lord of the forest, the mountains, the night

Lord of all predators, all the dark fright

Rend fear all failure, from mind body and heart

Make me a whole beast, then tear me apart!

Mate and devour me, birth and empower

Set my Wolf free, all fear to devour

By hoof, paws and fur, horns fangs and howl

I am one with the wildness, by moon-mother and owl

I leave skin of old shame, sin, sorrow and grief

In furred and clawed splendor, running wild with relief!

I lope among trees, just being in bliss,

Whole-mind intuition, free of abyss

O Lord of the Forest, wolf mountain and tree

I honor and call you, come set me free
I unleash All now, wildness awake in me!
Grant now my prayer
So mote it be!

Werewolf Power Candle Spell

There are no hard and fast rules to werewolf magick, it being a wild and animalistic magick that flows as unpredictably as winds and streams flow. Having a ready-to-use tool such as a werewolf power candle to help your magick when the wild wolf mood strikes you is useful. Fire magick is primal and such a candle offers quick werewolf magick when needed. It can be continually charged with sexual energy, blood, spit, and incantations, or during other werewolf magick practices, and can be used many times. The candle can be used to supercharge any werewolf magick mentioned in this book and it can be kept on your werewolf magick altar.

SETUP

It's best to use this spell at or near a full moon. Prepare a clean place that is also easy to clean, like a table or cleared off altar. It may be best to practice this spell outside on a small table; it will be more powerful and safer. Be aware of your surroundings and be mindful of what is near your candle.

There are two ways to make this candle: The easiest way is to get a "roll up" beeswax candle kit, with sheets of beeswax and a wick. You just add the herbs to the sheet, lay the wick, and tightly roll it up. Done. Or, if you have experience and wish to make a more traditional candle, you'll need candle making accessories, which can be found at a local hobby or craft store. You can make it with a candle mold or even in a ceramic cup or mug.

ITEMS NEEDED

A sacred and magickal knife

A small dish containing some of the herbal mix you will be using

A Pyrex container to melt the wax in (if you aren't making a roll-up candle)

A pot to fill with water

Sheets or cubes of wax and possibly other items from a hobby store depending on how you will make it

Various items depending on the kind of candle:

- Choose the color you wish: red, green, or black.
- Red for energetic shifting, wolf-power-boosting, help, or protection
- Green for healing, bonding, or werewolf magick of gain
- Black for working with the dead, protection, or attack

Items to scatter in the melted wax (or on the sheet of beeswax before you roll it up)

A bit of your hair

A bit of wolf, coyote, or dog hair, if possible

And, depending on what you want your candle to focus on, small amounts of these herbs:

- Red candle: Pepper flakes, a little ground up oak leaf, thistle, or rose petals
- Green candle: Rue, ground bay, rosemary, or sage
- Black candle: A very small amount of ground asafetida or black pepper, ground yarrow, ground up yew tree needles, or a bit of graveyard dirt.

The Spell

Create a small impromptu altar where you are making the candle. Assemble all the items on the altar and circle them all counterclockwise, using the knife to draw a circle of protection about it, growling:

Avert Avert Avert all that would interfere
This area is sacred, this altar is clear!
HA!

Powerfully and threateningly up-growl three times. Stand before the altar and do the Praxis Shifting Rite. Then, turn and circle the area three times clockwise and up-howl three times, shifting even more. Fully open your second sight and cast a glowing circle of white lunar power.

Then, burn some of the herbal mixture you will be using in your candle on the plate and bathe your head, heart, and groin in the smoke to purify yourself.

As you do so, do a low, quiet up-howl three times to invoke the blessing from the Lord of the Forest.

Raise your paws to the full moon and low up-howl three times, once for Artemis, once for Selene, once for Hekate. Bring that power down to the altar with open paws, then touch the earth and low up-howl three times for Gaia to bless this work.

Arms wide, embrace the Wildness, Wyrd, and Way and bark three times to call all the primordial powers to your wild wer work. Use spontaneous growl-words and werewolf lingo as you will—let it flow. Wave the smoke over the items assembled, growl the following words:

Charged and blessed by wolf-moon light
Arise wolf-power, open werewolf sight
By the Wyrd, Way and Wildness might
I conjure this cosmic werewolf light!
Unto the wolf! Spiritual light!

Began making the candle by either laying out the wax sheet or melting wax and adding the ingredients. Now, spit upon your right paw and rub it until it is fully wet.[60] Place the canine hairs in your palm, rub your paws together, and in a trance state see it as your own werewolf hair filled with your energy. Then put it on the wax sheet or add it to the melted wax with a low down-howl. As a wer, activate your solar plexus wolf-power center and let the fiery energy flow up into your body and out of your paws into the wax. Low up-growl and let the power of your wolf-self flow into it and see it glow with the color you have chosen for your candle. You may want to refer to the Wolf-Power Exercise in chapter 5 to enhance this work.

Clean your paws. Now sprinkle the appropriate ground items over your wax sheet or into your melted wax while deep down-growling the power into the candle. When done, add the wick and, depending on the kind of candle, either roll it up or carefully pour the wax and let it sit.

---

60. You may use blood or sexual fluids as well, depending on the candle and purpose.

Place your paws over the candle and rock back and forth; feel the wolf-power filling and flowing through your paws and into the candle. Howl repeatedly with each forward rock then finish by howling with your full force. Put your index finger to your lips, cutting off the power. See it glowing in the candle and being absorbed.

Let the wolf-power flow back down through your body and become calm as the energy calms in your solar plexus. When done, leave your candle in the full moon light for a time; sit and meditate on your intention.

When it has cooled and you feel it is ready, mark the wax with any sigil or glyphs you feel are appropriate, using the point of your ritual knife. You can refer to the sigils in chapter 3 or use whatever feels right to you and your Animalself.

When the candle is done, cooled, and ready to use, raise your paws and slowly up-howl three times with great ceremony, calling in this way the Wildness, Wyrd, and Way to bless this completed work. Light it.

Raise it up to the full moon and down-howl three times, once for Artemis, once for Selene, once for Hekate and "see" the moonlight fill it. Touch the base of the lit candle to the earth and do a low down-howl for Gaia as she fills the candle with power. Place it back on the altar.

Arms thrown wide, down-howl and call the Lord of the Forest and see the wild powers swirl and fix all the powers invoked into the candle. Blow out the flame and "see" all the energy sealed within the candle. Sway back and forth and rhythmically down-growl. Stomp your feet paws and add "MA" to each down-growl as your wer form fades and you return to being human.

Offer some of the leftover herbs and the excess energies to Gaia by sprinkling them on the earth. Then, scatter the last leftover ashes and herbs counterclockwise about the area with three low down-growls to banish. You are done. Keep the candle on your werewolf altar or at another sacred place for future use.

Werewolf Magick Lunar Holy Water Spell

With this spell you will create a werewolf magick holy water that can be used to protect, ward, cleanse, empower, and bless areas. Use your imagination. If you wish to keep your holy water for a long time, keep it in the fridge.

Werewolf magick is flexible and some might say it leans a bit more toward chaos than order. This is as it should be—being wild and unrestrained except by nature's patterns. Having certain items on hand, doing magickal work spontaneously, or changing how spells or rites are done is the norm for this magick. This werewolf holy water has many awesome wolfish superpowers and can be used in a bunch of different ways, as I'm sure you'll discover.

Setup

This spell should be done during a full or near full moon and when the sky is as clear as possible. Find a special natural sacred place with trees like a forest or other wild place. A yard will also do. You'll need a place where you can leave a glass container of water overnight in the moonlight. If you like, you can also use the triple moon sigil found in chapter 3 in any way you like to help focus the lunar energy.

Items Needed

Salt

A small pure white cloth, like a handkerchief

A large, sterile glass jar with a screw-on lid

A little pond or lake water

A little river, stream, or creek water

Water with sea salt in it *or* some ocean water

- Each type of water should be in a separate small, clean glass container
- All the waters should be gathered near the full moon, but can be collected on different days

A moonstone of any kind; it can even be inset on a silver ring or pendant

The Spell

On the night of the full moon before doing the spell, wash yourself with a bit of salt, and in silence go to your chosen sacred natural place. Set up a small altar, on a stone or stump if possible. Lay down the white cloth and place the empty glass jar, open, in the center with the three small glass jars with the three different waters in them. All of the jars together should form a downward pointing triangle. From top left, clockwise, in this order: lake water, river water, ocean water (or salty water.). Open the container of ocean/salty water and sprinkle some clockwise around the circle. Growl:

Out tout
Throughout and about
All evil stay out!
By Mara's fair
Saltwater hair
And silver air
MA!

Pick up the moonstone, anoint it with the salt water, use any werewolf lingo that feels right to you, and vibrate the sound "HA." Then carry it or wear it, depending on if it is loose or inset in jewelry. Do the Praxis Shifting Rite with the moonstone in your hand and awaken your wer "second sight" as you energize the moonstone.

Then, cast a magickal circle clockwise with the moonstone, now glowing with a white aura, while uttering three long, drawn out up-howls, deepening your wer trance. "See" the circle glowing with silver light as the moonstone is also glowing.

When done, hold the moonstone up to the full moon and down-howl three times, drawing down the moon power into the stone and circle, then low growl these words:

Elder moon mothers of space and sky
Artemis and Selene, to me fly
Come Hekate, open the silver eye!
IO IO IO!

Dunk the moonstone in each of the different waters, then place the stone in the open, empty, larger glass jar. Now hold up your paws over the altar and low down-howl "IO IO IO" over and over and see the swirling power of the

Moon Goddess in all her forms being "drawn down" into the items on the altar, all light focusing on the moonstone.

Pick up each small container of water and pour it in turn into the large jar, covering the moonstone. Start with the lake water, then pour in the river water, and finally the ocean water, each time up-howling as they blend and glow. Then growl the following:

From lunar snows to lake you flow
From lake through stream your powers grow
Streams join ocean where all things go
Come great moon magick, join and glow!

Now three times quietly down-howl the moon power into the large jar filled with the three joining, swirling, glowing now-united waters. Cap the jar, and growl the following:

Holy this be
by moon-mothers three!
Io Evoe, so mote it be
HAaaa

Put away the other containers, leave the jar with the now-holy moon water and immersed moonstone, put the lid firmly on it. Sit and meditate. Scry into the jar if you wish; it is a lunar gateway now. Growl, howl, bark as you like and take time to sit with the moon power. Werewolves love that moon, can't get enough!

When you're done and the energy has settled, down-growl, sway, and prowl counterclockwise three times slowly, firmly stepping on the earth as you leave the wer trance state and return to being human. Place your hands on the earth and keep down-growling, but add "MA" to the growls. Let it fade as Gaia embraces all the leftover lunar energy from her daughter Moon.

Finally, take a bit of the holy water from the large jar and sprinkle some on the earth, your head, heart, and loins and growl:

Great wild powers, now bless me
By wer magick and earth
Moon mothers and sea!
Holy water of rebirth
Of pure waters three
With moon power it grows
so may it be!
Aha!

Reach up and thank the moon, touch and honor the earth, throw your arms open and thank the Lord of the Forest, ground yourself, and go. Leave the tightly closed jar on the altar under the moonlight if you can or take it to a place where it can be moon-bathed, even if it is by a window.

The next morning gather up the jar and keep it well. Use the water as you need for werewolf magick work or for other kinds of magick. You can give vials of it to friends who need magickal help or mop your floor with some to cleanse and enchant your home; there are so many uses. The moonstone should be removed and worn or used for other werewolf magick work, for it is fully charged by lunar werewolf magick.

Attracting a Werewolf's Love Spell

Much of this book is about invoking and channeling werewolf magick to partake of the ecstasy of letting the primordial Animalself free to revitalize and empower your life. But, what if you're looking to bring such a werewolfish *person* to you? What if you're looking to hook a hot werewolf? After all, such a friend to have! Such a lover! Such a powerful ally! Why not? In the era of open relationships, furries, and varied sexuality, why should seeking a new friend with proverbial (or real) fur and fangs be neglected? Folklore says that certain flowers will actually attract a werewolf. The fact that such legends exist is proof that this romantic wish for werewolf love has been around for quite some time. And aren't we glad? Many love a furry feral bad boy or girl, and some apparently want them growling with bared fangs. If you are of this ilk, here is a spell for you.

SETUP

Following is a list of werewolf flowers that you need to find or buy fresh ahead of starting the spell. This spell should be done on a full moon when the sky is clear and the moon is shining in the sky. The spell says to keep the door to your home or bedroom unlocked, but that is up to you. Any decent werewolf should be able to leap up through your window. Some may prefer to wander through the woods while practicing this spell. If your goal is of a more intense personal nature, it would be best to also wear the scent of that flower. Just make sure it's natural; wers and wolves have sensitive snouts!

ITEMS NEEDED

"Werewolf flowers" of your choice. Mix and match as you like. These flowers could include:

- Lily of the Valley: for a deep werewolf friendship or romantic love
- Marigolds: for a werewolf partnership or interaction full of adventure and truth
- Red Azaleas: for attracting a werewolf of strong passions and emotions

THE SPELL

As you assemble the small werewolf-attracting bouquet on the sill of your open window, or as you are getting ready to go out roaming in the woods as the full moon rides the sky, sing the following traditional werewolf attraction spell:

"Oh softly come on shadow paws
With wine of longing and panting jaws
Fur of love and tail of bliss
Oh beast of desire, come for this!"[61]

End with a long, romantic, lilting up-howl or three. Do this for the three days of the full moon, and you'll see. An interesting person will come to thee.

---

61. O'Donnell, "Werewolves."

Have care and have fun; be carefree! (And watch those fangs, or a werewolf you'll be!)

An Abramelin Werewolf Spell

The purpose of this spell is to see if someone you know is a potential were-wolf friend. But first, a story. The magickal square, seen a few pages ahead in figure 15, is from the *Sacred Book of Abramelin the Mage*, supposedly written by a student of an Egyptian mage named Abra-Melin. He taught his unique eclectic system of magic to a Jewish occultist named Abraham of Worms, who lived in Germany from 1362 to 1458. The key item of interest in this curious book was the ritual known today as the "Knowledge and Conversation of the Holy Guardian Angel." Yet the book is also something of an occult mash-up that includes all sorts of other random spells with magickal spell-squares, including one to turn someone into a werewolf. I have reinterpreted this spell and com-posed a creative interpretation of what this spell should be.[62]

Setup

This spell should be practiced on a full moon night or close to full moon. Find a wooded or natural area that feels powerful to you. If you must do it inside, do it by a window with the moon shining down on the altar space you've cre-ated. If outside, find a stone or stump as an altar to do your work on. No mat-ter where you do this spell, face north if possible, with the full moon in the sky overhead.

Items Needed

Your magick knife

A red candle that has been blessed (the Werewolf Power Candle Spell earlier in this chapter would be perfect)

Dragon's blood ink that has been blessed and empowered with werewolf magick (see the blessing ritual in chapter 3)

A small brush or quill pen

An image of the Abramelin square to copy (see figure 15 on page 185)

---

62. *The Book of the Sacred Magic of Abramelin the Mage,* trans. Mathers, XV, 187–88.

A piece of natural parchment paper

A small red thread or ribbon

The Spell

Pick up the knife and walk with it counterclockwise, point out, up-growling eight times intensely to banish any unwanted energies in the space. Draw a pentagram over the assembled items with a ninth louder up-growl and then do the Praxis Shifting Rite.

When you are in a wer trance, stalk three times clockwise around your circle while low up-howling three times to cast a circle and call to the Lord of the Forest for aid. Then, light your candle while growling:

> By the power of the Lord of the Forest
> By the will of Faunus Lycan
> By the Moon Mother and the will of Wyrd
> This is a place now blessed and empowered
> L'chaim! ל'חיים[63]

Now, do a down-howl. Pull the powers of the forest and of Faunus Lycan into your circle as you enflame your solar plexus werewolf-power and fill your body.

At midnight, with the moon visible, sprinkle a few drops of the dragon's blood ink clockwise about the circle using the brush or quill. Growl the words that are in the Abramelin square from your copy, line by line.

Then, sit and draw/write out the Abramelin square with the magick ink on the parchment using your small brush or quill. Take your time, you don't want it messy. Down-growl with each letter written and see it glowing red as you do so with your wolf-power. As each line is done, intone that word in a deep growl. See the moon empower each word and make each one shine with eldritch power.

When you are done with the whole square, let it dry a bit and keep down-growling, using your wolf-power to make it glow brighter. When the

---

63. *To life!*

parchment has dried, hold it up to the moon, then growl all the words from top to bottom, bottom to top, from left vertical column to right, then from right vertical column to the left. When you're done, up-howl and see the square glowing even brighter than before. Lightly touch the parchment to the flame three times to seal the spell while saying:

אָדָם זְאֵב (ADAM-A-ZEV!)[64]

Blow out the candle. Sit in silence amidst the full moon light and let the charm fully dry. When it is completely dry and full of moon and fiery wolf-power, roll it up and tie it with the red thread or ribbon, up-growling to seal it. Thank the Lord of the Forest, Faunus Lycan, and the Moon Goddess with two gentle up-howls. Touch the spell scroll to the earth and thank Gaia with a third up-howl.

Clear the area completely. Silently walk counterclockwise once, letting the scroll absorb all the energy. Then walk around counterclockwise one more time, stomping in rhythm to your down-growls of "MA." Let the werewolf trance slip away into the Earth along with any leftover energy. Don't lose that scroll! Store it wisely., keep it handy.

Soon you will you meet a fellow wild one, maybe one who recognizes you as a fellow feral type. If your Animalself whispers *that one*, then offer to give him or her "the werewolf gift." If he or she says no, smile and move on. If he or she agrees, have them close their eyes, touch them lightly with the scroll and place it in their hands. Then you have to answer their questions and explain werewolf magick. See where it goes, maybe offer them a copy of this book.

If they are indeed amenable to werewolf magick, it will awaken their just stirring Animalself and you may soon have another werewolf friend to hang and howl with. It could even be the beginning of a pack! What will be will be. Lycanthropy: the gift that keeps on giving.

---

64. Translation for werewolf in Hebrew. (Yes, there is a legit word for werewolf in Hebrew.).

D	I	S	E	E	B	E	H
I	S	A	R	T	R	I	E
S	A	R	G	E	I	R	B
E	R	B	O	N	E	T	E
E	T	O	N	O	G	R	E
B	A	R	O	B	R	A	S
E	R	A	T	R	A	S	I
H	E	B	E	E	S	I	D

Figure 15: Abramelin Square

Eyes of the Wolf Spell

This simple magick spell turns on your "werewolf eyes" in order to either frighten an enemy or entrance and influence a human. However, this spell must never be used for coercion or with evil intent. It is a useful spell to protect yourself, avert injustice, or to let someone know your feelings of friendship or interest without words. Throughout history, the eyes of a werewolf were said to be full of power. Werewolves were said to be able to cast the "evil eye" and even entrance or glamour normal humans with their feral oracular powers.

Setup

This spell can be done anywhere at anytime but like many of the other spells, full moons offer the most power.

One thing you'll need for this spell is a red jasper stone, which should be charged up before doing the spell by using the blessing ritual in chapter 3. If you like, you can focus your power during the spell by also visualizing the Eye of Wolf sigil also found in chapter 3, but that is up to you.

Items Needed

A red jasper

Your bad-ass self

THE SPELL

Pick up the charged red jasper and carry it in your pocket when you feel you'll be in need of this wolf eye power. This charged stone is also a good general empowering talisman to have with you and will generally enhance all were-wolf magick. You can trigger "werewolf eyes'" to ward off or intimidate an aggressor or someone who is annoying. It can also be used to project an honest, "open" thought quite easily.

If someone is bullying you or a friend, or you are entering a sketchy situation, grab the stone in your hand and slightly shift by doing a quick version of the Praxis Shifting Rite, silently and internally.

Use the following steps when repelling danger or hostility: Do a deep, low rumble-growl in your chest and call up your Animalself while holding the jasper. Move your weight onto the balls of your feet, hunch over, and feel the werewolf energy rising up from your gut, through the stone in your hand and filling your eyes with red fire. Slightly grin and bare your fangs a little while staring at the person or other source of danger. "See" red and feel your eyes flashing crimson. Let the force and fire of your powerful gaze strike the person and then reflect the negativity back. Keep growling very low in your chest. If necessary, become more wolfish.

Avoid all talking or arguing; let your blazing eyes speak for you. If you must speak in this situation, use simple one word answers like "no" or "go." The effect will often be fairly immediate and as the heat or your "wolf gaze" hits them, they will often recoil a bit and go. If not, practice your "wolf gaze."

For silently communicating honest feelings: If you are doing this to communicate true feelings to someone, dial back the previous directions a bit. No one likes an overbearing wolf. Lightly shape-shift as mentioned, hold the jasper, and let the less-fiery power rise through the stone in your hand to your heart and from your heart through your eyes. This time, share a warm smile without showing too many teeth! Focus on your simple feeling of caring, friendship, or polite interest. Nonverbal communication is always more honest. The person or people you are looking at may stop speaking, alter their conversation, or may actually step closer and meet your gaze and speak with you. If they respond to your gaze, good. If not, leave it. Whatever you were communicating may not be their will.

When you're finished, lower this reddish werewolf power, pull it down into your gut fire center and breathe deeply. Put the red jasper down and very quickly down-growl to come back to your full human-self before engaging with anyone else. When you're finished with the spell, wash the stone with cool running water to remove excess energy.

Spell to Make Someone Shut Up

Old legends and stories about werewolves say that if a human is out at night and a werewolf locks eyes with them, the werewolf will cause the human to lose the ability to speak and their vocal cords will be paralyzed. Here is a spell to use your werewolf eyes to simply silence a bigmouth, or to at least get them to stop yacking at you.

Figure 16: Isa Rune

SETUP

This spell can be done anywhere, but it's best to prepare yourself a few minutes beforehand. You should also be familiar with the Norse rune Isa, which is a simple straight line, as seen in figure 16.

This rune represents ice, stasis, or silence and it has the added power of using silence as a way to gain wisdom or awareness, something the person you want to shut up could use.

ITEMS NEEDED

Your wolfy self

The Isa rune

The Spell

When approaching or being approached by a mouthy, loud, obnoxious, or just inanely talkative person you wish to avoid, follow these steps: Do a very quick and silent mental version of the Praxis Shifting Rite with very subtle swaying. Bring up the wolf-power from your gut to your eyes. Go up on the balls of your feet, arms slightly out, breathe deeply with a low, very quiet rumble growl and present a blank, emotionless frozen face.

Visualize your face morphing into a wolfish form, and your body increasing in size and strength. As you stand before the jabbering, trolling, or yelling person, very quietly, deep in your chest, growl the sound "eeeee." While growling, visualize the Isa rune as a glowing, icy white vertical line across that person's lips, holding them shut. Let your wolf-power flow into it. Don't overdo it, you just want them to stop talking, not get laryngitis.

If they are determined to keep yacking, casually put your hand-paw to your chin and place your index finger over your lips. This is the sign of silence and the Isa rune. Do not talk; use nonverbal communication like a nod, smile, or frown. In a short time, if they haven't already left you, their chatting will slow and stop. Smile and move on.

Breath deeply three times and see the Isa rune you projected melt and dissolve into the air along with your irritation. As you walk away, sway a bit and let the wolf-power fall back asleep within you and then into the earth as you return to a human state.

If you really want this person to not speak to you anymore at all, do this spell three times. They will avoid you. This spell can also be done with a photo of someone who is spreading rumors about you. Just draw the Isa rune over their mouth in silver or white and destroy the photo when they stop.

Werewolf Berserker Spell

Use this spell if you ever feel the need for special warrior empowerment, whether in business, academia, or in actual fighting. With it you can call upon the werewolf magick to help you "armour up" and be your biggest bad ass werewolf self. In the ancient days, elite VIking warriors before battle would call upon their wolfish god Odin and a seidr or sorcerer to grant them special werewolf shifting power. This power would help them become a "berserker," or a wolfskin-covered fighter filled with divine animalistic power, strength, and skill. This power would also give the fighters phenomenal tolerance for pain and quick healing powers, or so the sagas say.

Figure 17: Berserker Rune

Setup

Go to a natural place or find a secluded spot near one big, strong tree. Prepare a sterilized pin or sharp ritual knife to prick yourself for blood, unless you are going to use spit. Memorize the berserker rune, seen above as figure 17, ahead of time. Do this on a waxing to full moon night or day. Set aside twenty minutes—you'll need some time alone before your "battle."

Items Needed

A pin or pointy, sharp ritual knife

Some pure salt

Your werewolf talisman

The Spell

Shower or bathe with a pinch of salt and mentally banish all fears and distractions before you head out into your natural area. Head to your natural place in silence and find a special place of calm and power under a large tree filled with energy. If you can, take off your shoes and socks. Your shirt too, if acceptable. Inhale and feel the Earth around you and under you, full of life. Touch the tree with both palms and take some deep breaths; let all negativity and doubt flow into it as you exhale and let that be replaced by green calm within you every time you inhale. Breathe deeply, low growl quietly, and feel your body and your Animalself.

In your mind, surround yourself with a circle of glowing energy. Feel your protective and aggressive martial energy rise as you focus completely on what challenging situation you must soon face and conquer. Low up-howl, open your arms, and invoke the Lord of the Forest in your heart. Put on your werewolf talisman. Do the Praxis Shifting Rite quietly or, if it is a public place, silently.

"See" yourself become a large werewolf warrior as your swaying and growls deepen, carrying a large ax or sword with powerful claws. Tap into your fire gut center and fill your werewolf self with flames of power to help build up this mental image of your werewolf berserker self until you feel it is you.

When you are this kick-ass werewolf warrior, up-howl with all your wer muscles straining. Take the pin or knife and *carefully* prick your finger (you may use spit instead). Use the blood (or spit) to draw the berserker rune on your chest or the top of your right foot while growling the following:

Vargur, Vargur, Vargur![65]

Then, low down-howl to the Earth and wear the energy. As the blood (or spit) dries, feel all the werewolf energy of the circle you have created contract into a red glow filling the bloody rune on your body until it glows. Lean back on the trec and let the spell settle, with low rumble-growling. When the blood dries, go forth to a sure victory in whatever trial awaits you!

When done, thank your Animalself for filling you with werewolf power and courage as you slowly take a swaying walk after your event. As you do so low down-growl in time with your steps and feel the wolf power and your werewolf trance fade and sink into the earth. Wash off the bloody rune while offering the reddish water with thanks to Gaia, the Lord of the Forest, and the Wolf Spirit.

---

65. "Wolf" in Icelandic.

The berserker wolf spirit sleeps in your heart and can always be a deep part of you, a wolfish warrior self. It can always be called up in the future by shifting and visualizing this rune glowing red in your heart when facing challenges.

Popping Claws Protection Spell

This spell is very different from the previous spell. Rather than fighting, this spell is about avoiding altercations and fights and creating a shield of protection or cloak of stealth so you can avoid problems by being a dangerous shadow wer. This could also be called ninja werewolf magick spell. If you need to project a "Do not mess with me!" vibe, then you need to "pop your claws," which wolves do when they're preparing to attack or defend. You will invoke respect and maybe a bit of fear with this spell. This spell will include a new idea we haven't talked about yet: shape-shifting specific parts of our bodies. In this spell you will be shape-shifting just your hands and arms.

Setup

If you find yourself in a negative situation or you know you're approaching one, find a quiet place to practice this spell. Set aside a few minutes of quiet to concentrate and gather your courage.

Items Needed

Just your ninja werewolf self and clean hands

The Spell

When in the quiet place you've chosen, breathe deeply, gather your courage, and face east if possible. Do a long, low up-growl intensely but quietly three times, each time whispering the following:

Loup-Garou
Arise In Me
As I Will
So May It Be!

Take a minute to subtly do a very fast version of the Praxis Shifting Rite in your mind and when you start to feel and "see" the astral fur, muscles, and bones shift, halt it part-way and do this: Focus all your shape-shifting power to your hands and eyes. Draw up flaming wolf-power from your gut and send it just to your hands and eyes. See just your hands and face glow with red power and transform into a partial wer form. Focus on your tingling, glowing hand-paws.

Hold your left paw out before you, palm up, fingers extended. With your right paw, palm down, fingers extended, touch the bunched nails of your right hand to the palm of the left hand. Now, trace those five fingernails slowly up each finger of the left hand, one nail tracing along each finger, all at once, like a flower opening. As you do so, feel glowing energy tingle in the center of the palm being touched and flow up each finger. "See" sparks running up the fingers of the left hand as the half-paws morph into huge furry paws with long, extended, deadly claws! As you do this, whisper:

Wolf, wolf, I extend my claws!

Switch hands and do the exact same thing to the right hand with the left hand. Repeat the same chant:

Wolf, wolf, I extend my claws!

Now, stand up tall. With a wide, powerful stance, open your arms, palms up, claws popped and splayed. Arch your back and "see" your eyes wolfishly glowing red, then whisper:

Oh god, a werewolf!
(deep up-growling)
I am a werewolf!

Up-growl and do your ninja werewolf thing as you face your challenge. Use a lot of hand gestures and pointing to increase the emotional impact of your astral popped werewolf claws. Flipping someone off is especially cutting.

Later on, when your popped claws are not needed, simply reverse the finger stroking actions, from tips to center of palm, and "withdraw the claws." Take a moment to let the wolf-power flow back into your gut and then down into the earth with a long down-growl of "MA." As your werewolf power and adrenaline subside, whisper:

I am not a werewolf ... now ...

Breathe deeply; let all the stress sink into the ground as your wolf retreats and smile. You are indeed a badass ninja wolf.

Lunar Eclipse Purification Spell

Several times a year the full moon is devoured by what some legends see as a great wolf spirit, which changes the lunar sphere red as blood and all goes dark as the spirit eats it. Lunar eclipses are powerful and in werewolf magick, they mark a time of release, letting go, and purification. As you are developing and expanding your werewolf form, the process is enhanced and sped up by letting go of those spiritual and psychological hindrances, restrictions, and flaws that suppress your Animalself. Eclipses are gifts given by the Moon Goddess so that we may bathe in the red lunar eclipse power and thus dissolve hindrances and restrictions to our wer will.

Setup

Find a wild and secluded place to view the lunar eclipse, free of people and electric lights. Watch the timing! Arrive under the full moon as the eclipse begins.

Items Needed

Just your werewolf self and a lunar eclipse

The spell

Walk in a small circle around the area where you will be stationed for the whole eclipse and up-growl nine times to free the area of other unwanted energies. Announce yourself and offer praise to the full moon by up-howling three times, arms open and raised. Feel the lunar power embrace you as you "hold" it in your hands. Touch the Earth and see the moon power creating a silver circle about you as you down-howl. Do the Praxis Shifting Rite. Continue swaying and low down-growling until the moon is partially eclipsed. Rise up and "hold" the shifting moon in your cupped paws and growl:

> Great wolf eclipse!
> Remove my human problems!
> Honor to the wolf moon!

Stand with open arms and embrace the rays of the red moon as they fill your wer self and pass through your dissolving human consciousness. Let it wash away all restrictions, insecurities, neuroses, and programming you want to let go of. Banish all that restricts your Animalself. When the moon is at full eclipse, chant-growl:

> Oh glorious wolf eclipse Moon!
> Bless and empower me!
> As the great wolf devours the Moon
> So my restrictions are devoured!

Let go, let go, *let it all go* … then up-howl. As the eclipse begins to end and the true moon is almost fully emerged, be still in your wer form. Then, quietly sway, stomp your feet, and lower your arms while low down-growling "MA" over and over. Feel all you have let go, as well as your werewolf powers, flow into the earth, returning you to human form.

As the eclipse finishes, raise your hands into the air to the Moon Goddess above and growl-chant the following:

By the wolf god Faunus, so be it!

Clap three times, then up-howl a big thank you. Afterward, go to sleep. The next day you will feel a bit psychologically and physically raw, but happier and freer than you were.

CONCLUSION

THE FINAL HOWL

L et me begin with a true story. The Yellowstone park ecosystem, which was in steep decline, was saved by the reintroduction of wolves. The wolves, which had lived there for eons, were killed off in the early twentieth century by humans. Overpopulation of elk herds soon followed, decimating the foliage in the park and thus the habitats for numerous other species. The whole environment unraveled. Wolves were reintroduced and protected in 1995 and a miracle of regeneration happened. It was shockingly rapid and indicated that the whole ecosystem was linked to the wolf population and its control over other species, like elk. All the animals, fish, and plant species returned and flourished within a fairly short time. The wolves reset the ecological balance of a whole ecosystem because they were the apex predators—until human predators eliminated them out of fear and ignorance. This kind of ignorance and arrogance is why we are on the edge of an ecological catastrophe today. It also brings me to the key ethos behind werewolf magick: *We must consciously rejoin our ecosystem, we must own our responsibilities and awareness as apex predators.* We must regain the instincts of wolves and live consciously within nature or else we'll continue to destroy nature beyond repair. Our Animalself is the key to this.

Our ecosystem is the crucial magick that surrounds our lives. As a species we have shredded the web of life about us, taking and building and poisoning thoughtlessly. We continue to decimate our wild animal kin, thus endangering ourselves, because they are our spirit guides, our ancestors, our teachers, *our kin*. We have lost our way and forgotten our true selves. We must remember who we are. This book is all about remembering.

All significant change must begin with remembering that we too are animals within nature. This is where awareness and magick become crucial. For the last thousand or so years we have been programmed into believing that we are the rulers of the Earth and that it is ours to do with as we will. Many religions preach that we are the masters of all living things and are the only living creature with a soul. This falsehood is the root of our madness, arrogance, and thoughtless excessive consumption of nature.

Werewolf magick offers one of the oldest and deepest answers to this nightmare. An act of helping nature, such as reintroducing wolves, can have astounding effects on our environment, just as simple acts of helping ourselves can cause magickal effects all around us. If we each awaken our Animalself and remember and utilize our Instinct, Intuition, and Insight, we can change the world. This subsuming of materialistic arrogance and superiority is not an easy task and means letting go of much of our civilized programming, but we need to embrace this process if we are to survive as a species.

One of our werewolf magick goals is to reintroduce Animalself consciousness into the spiritual ecology of the overly abstract and intellectual esoteric world by owning our Animalself in our lives. As with the regimen of shamans, this takes a lot of wildness work but offers the freedom of rejoining nature-consciousness as a member, not invader. A secret to realizing this primal magick is painted on prehistoric cave walls, showing that we merge with nature when we use magick to become a human/animal, in our case, a "wer-wulf" or werewolf. Such shape-shifting is a powerful magick many cultures have always had. With this reality shift, we can each fulfill our role in our ecosystem with awareness and humble gratitude.

Werewolf magick emerged as a trigger for this shift in consciousness, a visceral, feral, and intense one. It is unlike most other Western magick, the goal being to suppress the intellect and ego and unleash our primal beast-self, our lower cortex "animal mind." This "de-intellectualization" is somewhat contrary to most occult teachings, but opens the door to reveling in our senses, powers, and subliminal awareness that only our inner animal has access too. It's time to return to the animalistic rituals, practices, revels, and wildness within nature that bring deep and powerful joy, practices that our culture has all but forgotten.

When we do the work of werewolf magick, we embody the timeless and ancient archetype of the shape-shifter werewolf, the animal-man, the shaman who listens to and understands the whispers of the forest animals, of the earth, and the songs of the moon and stars.

We who have embraced werewolf magick *really know this:* we are smart, feral, amazing beasts who can dress in a suit for work and later that night run naked and howling in the woods under the moon. This is real spiritual freedom. This is real visceral life. This is remembering.

A Final Werewolf Magick Wrap-Up

We began with my wild tale of losing everything and finding the Wildness and the Wolf Spirit, almost by accident, amidst the carnage of my life as a way of pointing out that experimenting, exploring, researching, and peeling away all restrictive programming is not always a pleasant transformation, but is crucial to werewolf magick.

We unwound the myths and legends of werewolf magick, following in the footsteps of ancient historians and modern researchers to understand that werewolf magick, by many names, began with our ancient ancestors and wove through many ancient civilizations, eventually influencing medieval witch shape-shifters who were so brutally suppressed. Now, in the present, we rediscovered the ethos and pragmatics behind all werewolf magick embodied in the Wildness, Wyrd, and Way and the feral superpowers of Instinct, Intuition, and Insight. We then began to shift to a more feral point of view and how to reach back into the depths of our primal being, to speak with howls and growls and so give voice to our Animalself. The wolfishness within us grew until our inner wolf stirred, stretched, growled, and opened its eyes and we embraced and unleashed our werewolf self with a leap and howl, soon mastering the shape-shift from human to werewolf with ease. Best of all, we embraced and are embraced by nature as a natural and powerful part of the ecosystem, a conscious animal, at one with Gaia.

So we are now werewolf magick practitioners, true werewolves and shape-shifters, able to perform the feral rituals, rites, and spells, work with our Double and Fetch in several ways, speak to the dead, and open up doors that are closed to simple humans. As we transform ourselves we find that proficiency in shape-shifting also shifts perceptions in expansive and positive ways because experiencing the world with feral consciousness opens a new world of primal spirit and power. With these shifts, we can craft our own rituals and spells as our inner wolf guides us.

Here we are, my newly born werewolf friends, at the ritual crossroads between worlds, in the great eternal dark primal forest, a liminal place of natural magick. Feel the full moon overhead. Together we shift, growling, rocking as the claws, fangs, and fur emerge from our powerful bodies and all our senses sharpen. The stars glitter above us and our fellow nocturnal animals scurry and give voice about us. Together we rise on furred haunches and splayed paws, sniffing the air full of pine and creek mist and ancient powers. We feel the Wyrd, the spirits, the flow of all things.

We howl together: we are home.

Werewolf magick is really just the beginning of your prowling journey. It is an initiation into Wildness, a freeing of restrictions and a healthy organic shock to complacent, civilized, intellectual occultism. A visceral shift into the feral consciousness of Animalself taps the real source of primordial power and joy and is needed now more than ever.

Our wild gods are not spiritual metaphors or cosmic entities, they are the dirt beneath our naked paws, the rain that tastes sweet on our tongues, the lunar dance of the tides within us and the fresh scented air of spring that fills us with green energy. Gaia is not abstract; we pray to her with every step we take, with everything we eat with gratitude, and with every leap of our amazing body. Werewolf magick, like all ancient and primal magicks, is primarily of the body and the things of nature. It is all we need. When we truly embrace our Animalself and integrate it, we shape-shift into a more deeply powerful and satisfying relationship with divinity and nature, and realize that *this is the truth of who we are*. And so we return to the ancient truth that the animals and trees are our brothers and sisters, our ancestors, our gods, ourselves. When we truly live this truth, then we have awakened and we become the new wolves reintroduced into a damaged ecosystem who, *by our very presence and natural actions*, revives and renews all about us by being the divine animals we are.

It is my deepest and most sincere hope and feral prayer that werewolf magick has helped each of us to wear our "true skin" and discard the old, tired, and torn bindings that restricted our Animalselves. I pray our shape-shifting magick is strong and that we all walk with the Wildness amidst the Wyrd as we follow our true Way.

You, oh newly born werewolf, are all of these incarnate and will be for all eternity. This is the real truth of shape-shifting, the nature and transformation is eternal! HA!

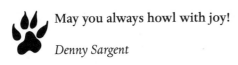 May you always howl with joy!

Denny Sargent

A Blessing for All Your Werewolf Magick Work

May Artemis Wolf Mother protect you,
May Selene of the Full-Luna Light empower you,
May Hekate, Three-Wolf Matron of all Mystery guide you
May the Lord of the Forest grant you the Instinct, Intuition and Insight
That you may work and play in wildness, safely and with joy
May Gaia always rise up under your feet and bless you
When you dance as your beautiful Beast-Self the Under the Stars!
Aha.

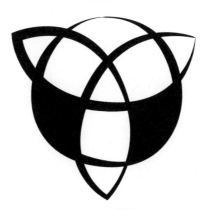

Figure 18: Wolf Triquetra

APPENDIX A

A THEORETICAL RECONSTRUCTION OF A MEDIEVAL FULL-TRANSFER SHAPE-SHIFTING RITUAL

————————— ┼┼┼ —————————

The most extreme form of shape-shifting with the Double is purely theoretical at this point. I call it "full-transfer shape-shifting." It is supposedly accomplished by the transfer of the werewolf sorcerer's full consciousness, or soul, out of their body and into the wolf-shaped wolf Double or Fetch, thus rendering the physical body comatose. The werewolf goes forth as a separate entity in the actual physical world with the mind and soul of the sorcerer. If this "solidified werewolf body" is hurt, the empty physical human body also becomes injured. One author describes this as "the sending forth of the 'Fetch' in lupine shape by night during the ecstatic trance in which the body lies in cataleptic death-like slumber, constitutes the inner secret."[66]

There are so many firsthand historical accounts of this kind of real, physical werewolf shape-shifting that we cannot completely discount them all. There was almost always the same basic pattern: A werewolf appeared and attacked livestock or people. It was described as being bigger than a wolf and when it was shot with an arrow or gun, *it would immediately disappear!* Often, later on, a person in a nearby village would be discovered with the *exact same wounds inflicted on the werewolf.* I have already related a number of these accounts earlier in this book.

---

66. Jackson, *The Compleat Vampyre: The Vampyre Shaman, Werewolves, Witchery & the Dark Mythology of the Undead*, 144.

These are examples of "full-transfer shape-shifting" where the Double was made so powerful and "familiar" through years of practice, that the soul of the accomplished sorcerer could *fully enter the werewolf Double* which became an independent entity that could be seen and physically interact with others. In many ways this is just a final step from the shape-shifting we have done in this book, but more dangerous of course. Intentionally putting oneself into a coma is no laughing matter and could be fatal. It should be left to master shamans with years of experience and training. It would be foolhardy to try such an operation, but it is fascinating to see what others may have done in the past and so I include it here.

Most anything you want out of shape-shifting doesn't require a coma; using what this book offers gives you all the tools you need to reach your goals. However, I feel compelled to at least offer this hypothetical reconstruction of what such a ritual may have looked like for historical and informational purposes only. The following hypothetical ritual is based on several fragmentary sources and thus has lost its exactitude.

A Hypothetical Reconstruction Procedure to Become a Physical Werewolf

To begin, a sorcerer needed a quiet, secure place to do the lengthy ritual. Some texts say a crypt was ideal so one wouldn't be discovered as they completed the next steps.

Invocation of the Lord of the Werewolves: Several documents called this being "the dark man" or "the devil." The emphasis was on names the sorcerer was familiar with. It is unclear whether this was done spontaneously or was a rite that was prepared and read aloud.

Invocation of the werewolf stars: The next stage seems to have been about invoking stellar wolf powers to aid in the transformation through the stars associated with the wolf-power. In one version a "star pentacle" was to be present, but what it was like is unknown.

Sacrifice to the werewolf stars: Again, it is unclear what this sacrifice was. It seems a chaotic werewolf god was somehow connected with star entities or power.

Anointing with the werewolf salve: The next step generally seemed to consist of rubbing a psychoactive werewolf shifting salve or potion on to the body.

Ritually putting on the wolfskin: A wolfskin or wolfskin belt seems to have been put on with great ceremony. The sorcerer would then utter oaths and spells to evoke and manifest the werewolf Double.

Shaking the soul loose or "seething": This seems to have involved "shaking" the soul out of the body. Norse seidr or sorcery offers techniques for this. Such self-induced shaking is also a shamanic technique.

Leaving the human body: The sorcerer's soul then left the body and shifted to the evoked werewolf Double with the help of the Lord of Werewolves.

The final calling to the Werewolf God: The Werewolf God would then urge, push, or whip the sorcerer's soul, pushing it out of the human body into a whirlwind of chaos, until…

The leap into the werewolf Double: The soul or the sorcerer then leapt into the empowered astral werewolf-Double. It's unclear where exactly the werewolf-sorcerer went and what he or she did. The body, meanwhile, lay comatose in a safe place.

The return to the human body: When the sorcerer was done with the wolfy travels, he or she returned to the human body and let go of the werewolf-Double form before daybreak.

The return to the human-self: The sorcerer ate and drank, took off the belt, got warm and began to move his or her stiff and cold body about, and likely did some final ritual work. It is hard to know what exactly they did to finish the ritual, but for sure that sorcerer would have had a hell of a shape-shifting hangover.

Takeaways

Much of this theoretical full-transfer werewolf ritual is based on medieval and Slavic historical and occult sources. There are a number of interesting archaic elements in the fragments I've assembled and the primal and chaotic Werewolf God seems to be in sync with the Lord of the Forest we have come to know. Some aspects of this ritual evoking/invoking fusion are similar to some shamanic rituals I've learned from. The drumming and chanting for hours, the induced teeth-rattling shaking or seething, and the intense single pointed focus of will are not uncommon in serious shamanic and occult ritual work, nor is the use of psychoactive substances. The wolf stars and other embedded star lore in this reconstituted ritual is fascinating. It deserves much more research and study and hearkens to ancient stellar magick. Finally, it's often noted in sources that such werewolves had to take several days to recover from such journeys, and the same has been said to me by the shamans I studied with. One can only imagine!

BIBLIOGRAPHY

Books

Adkins, Lesley and Roy A. Adkins. *Dictionary of Roman Religion*. Oxford: Oxford University Press, 2000.

Agrippa, Henry Cornelius. *His Fourth Book of Occult Philosophy: Of Geomancy; Magical Elements of Peter De Abano; Astronomical Geomancy; The Nature Of Spirits, Arbatel of Magick*. Fayetteville, TN: Askin Publishers, 1978.

Baring-Gould, Sabine. *The Book of Werewolves*. London: Smith, Elder & Co., 1865. Reprinted, London: Studio Editions, 1995.

Betz, Hans Dieter, ed. *The Greek Magical Papyri in Translation*. Chicago: The University of Chicago Press, 1986.

Brewer, E.C. *Dictionary of Phrase & Fable*. London: Wordsworth Editions, 2006.

The Book of the Sacred Magic of Abramelin the Mage. Translated by MacGregor Mathers. New York: Dover, 1975.

Carr-Gomm, Philip. *The Book of English Magic*. New York: Hodder & Stoughton, 2014.

Conway, D. J. *Magickal, Mythical, Mystical Beasts: How to Invite Them into Your Life*. Woodbury, MN: Llewellyn Publications, 1996.

Cooper, J.C. *Symbolic & Mythological Animals*. Northampton, UK: The Aquarian Press, 1992.

Curran, Bob. *Werewolves: A Field Guide to Shapeshifters, Lycanthropes, and Manbeasts*. Franklin Lakes, NJ: New Page Books, 2009.

Fitzgerald, Robert. *Arcanum Bestiarum*. Richmond Vista, CA: Three Hands Press, 2012.

Fries, Jan. *Cauldron of the Gods: A Manual of Celtic Magick*. Oxford, UK: Mandrake, 2003.

———. *Seidways: Shaking, Swaying and Serpent Mysteries*. Oxford, UK: Mandrake of Oxford, 2010.

Frowhen, Mornaem. *Saxon Northumbrian Pagan Runes*. Seattle, WA: Catweasel Productions, 1980.

Gary, Gemma. *Traditional Witchcraft: a Cornish Book of Ways*. London: Troy Books, 2012.

Godfrey, Linda S. *Real Wolfmen: True Encounters in Modern America*. London: Penguin Group, 2012.

Grant, Kenneth. *Nightside of Eden*. London: Starfire Publishing, 2014.

Graves, Zachary. *Werewolves*. New York: Chartwell Books, 2011.

Griffiths, Bill. *Aspects of Anglo-Saxon Magic*. Norfolk, UK: Anglo Saxon Books, 2012.

Izzard, Jon. *Werewolves*. New York: Spruce, 2009.

Jackson, Nigel. *The Compleat Vampyre: The Vampyre Shaman, Werewolves, Witchery & the Dark Mythology of the Undead*. Somerset, UK: Capall Bann, 1995.

Johnson, Buffie. *Lady of the Beasts: the Goddess and Her Sacred Animals*. Rochester, VT: Inner Traditions International, 1994.

Jung, Carl G. *Man and His Symbols*. New York: Anchor Press Doubleday, 1988.

Knowles, Elizabeth. *Oxford Dictionary of Phrase and Fable*. Oxford: Oxford University Press, 2016.

Leach, Maria and Jerome Fried, eds. *Funk & Wagnalls Standard Dictionary of Folklore, Mythology, and Legend*. New York: Harper Collins, 1972.

Lecouteux, Claude. *Witches, Werewolves, and Fairies: Shapeshifters and Astral Doubles in the Middle Ages*. Rochester, VT: Inner Traditions, 2003.

Lupa. *Fang and Fur, Blood and Bone: a Primal Guide to Animal Magic*. Stafford, UK: Megalithica Books, 2006.

McHargue,Georgess. *Meet the Werewolf.* New York: Dell, 1983.

Morgan, Lee. *A Deed Without a Name: Unearthing the Legacy of Traditional Witchcraft.* Winchester, UK: Moon Books, 2013.

Ronnberg, Ami and Kathleen Martin, eds. *The Book of Symbols: Reflections on Archetypal Images.* Cologne, Germany: Taschen, 2010.

Sagan, Carl. *Cosmos.* New York: Ballantine, 2013.

Spence, Lewis. *An Encyclopaedia of Occultism.* New York: Cosimo Classics, 2006.

Steiger, Brad. *The Werewolf Book: The Encyclopedia of Shape-Shifting Beings.* Canton, MI: Visible Ink Press, 2012.

Summers, Montague. *The Werewolf.* Secaucus, NJ: Citadel Press, 1973.

Telesco, Patricia. *Dog Spirit: Hounds, Howlings, and Hocus Pocus.* Rochester, VT: Park Street Press, 2000.

Walker, Barbara G. *The Woman's Dictionary of Symbols and Sacred Objects.* London: Pandora, 1995.

———. *The Woman's Encyclopedia of Myths and Secrets,* San Francisco: HarperOne, 1983.

Wickwar, John William. *Witchcraft and the Black Art: a Book Dealing with the Psychology and Folklore of the Witches.* London: Herbert Jenkins Limited, 1923.

Zell-Ravenheart, Oberon. *A Wizard's Bestiary.* Franklin Lakes, NJ: New Page Press, 2007.

E-books

Franklin, Alberta Mildred. "Chapter 3 – The Wolf-Deity in Greece" in *The Lupercalia.* New York, 1921. http://penelope.uchicago.edu/Thayer/E/Roman/Texts/secondary/FRALUP/3*.html.

———. "Chapter 4 – The Wolf-Deity in Italy" in *The Lupercalia.* New York, 1921. http://penelope.uchicago.edu/Thayer/E/Roman/Texts/secondary/FRALUP/4*.html.

Frazer, James George. "Pausanias and His Description of Greece," The Project Gutenberg EBook of Studies in Greek Scenery, Legend and History." Gutenberg. Accessed 2011. https://www.gutenberg.org /files/56002/56002-h/56002-h.htm.

O'Donnell, Elliot. "Werewolves." The Athenaeum. October 12, 1912, no. 4433, p. 410. Digitized in 2017 by the University of Wisconsin. Originally published at the Office, Bream's Buildings, Chancery Lane in London. https:// books.google.com/books?id=hx8RwggCztsC&dq=lily+of+the+valley,+marigolds+and+azaleas+are+said+to+attract+werewolves.&source=gbs_navlinks_s.

Pausanias. *Description of Greece*. Translated by Sir J. G. Frazer. London: MacMillan and Co., 1917. https://www.gutenberg.org/files/56002/56002-h/56002-h.htm.

Websites

All That's Interesting. "The Grisly Werewolf Panic That Swept Europe a Century Before the Salem Witch Trials." All That's Interesting. Last modified October 14, 2019. https://allthatsinteresting.com/hans-werewolf-trials.

Ancient-Symbols.com. "Triquetra Symbol." Ancient-Symbols.com. Accessed 2019. https://www.ancient-symbols.com/symbols-directory/triquetra .html.

Beloved in Light: Following the Path of Apollon. "Of Dogs and Wolves." Beloved in Light: Following the Path of Apollon. Last modified on February 1, 2012. https://lykeiaofapollon.wordpress.com/2012/02/01/of-dogs-and -wolves/.

Bettini, Jessica Lynne. "The Rage of the Wolf: Metamorphosis and Identity in Medieval Werewolf Tales." Medievalists.net. Last modified April 2013. https://www.medievalists.net/2013/04/the-rage-of-the-wolf -metamorphosis-and-identity-in-medieval-werewolf-tales/.

Canfield, Nicole. "Wolf Gods and Goddesses." Otherworldly Oracle. Last modified June 1, 2018. https://otherworldlyoracle.com/wolf-gods-wolf -goddesses/.

The Complementary Medical Association. "Werewolves: A Medical Perspective." The Complementary Medical Association. Last modified 2012. https://www.the-cma.org.uk/Articles/Werewolves-a-medical-perspective-3791/.

EROCx1 Blog. "Terrence McKenna: The Ethnobotany of Shamanism." EROCx1 Blog. Last modified July 9, 2009. http://erocx1.blogspot.com/2009/06/terence-mckenna-ethnobotany-of.html.

Garrett-Hatfield, Lori. "Animals That Share Human DNA Sequences." Seattle Pi. Accessed in 2019. https://education.seattlepi.com/animals-share-human-dna-sequences-6693.html.

Hance, Jeremy,. "Egyptian Jackal is Actually Ancient Wolf." Mongabay. Last modified January 26, 2011. https://news.mongabay.com/2011/01/egyptian-jackal-is-actually-ancient-wolf/.

Häussler, Ralph. "Wolf-Mythology-Celtic." Ralph Häussler. Last modified 2016. https://ralphhaussler.weebly.com/wolf-mythology-celtic.html.

———. "Wolf-Mythology-Greek." Ralph Häussler. Last modified 2016. https://ralphhaussler.weebly.com/wolf-mythology-greek.html.

———. "Wolf-Mythology-Italy." Ralph Häussler. Last modified 2016. https://ralphhaussler.weebly.com/wolf-mythology-italy.html.

Hedeager, Ulla, "Is Language Unique to the Human Species?," Semantic Scholar, 2003. https://pdfs.semanticscholar.org/3611/9d61cab921fd01f9e961c32ba28474a3aabd.pdf.

Hieroglyphs.net. "Dictionary." Hieroglyphs.net. Accessed 2019. http://hieroglyphs.net/cgi/dictionary_lookup.pl?ty=en&ch=e&cs=0.

Hoffman, Mark, "Huichol Wolf Shamanism." The Nagual. Last modified January 18, 2012. https://www.tapatalk.com/groups/sorcery/huichol-wolf-shamanism-t3567.html.

Koosmen, Tanika. "The Ancient Origins of Werewolves." The Conversation. Last modified October 28, 2018. https://theconversation.com/the-ancient-origins-of-werewolves-104775.

Lewis-Williams, David, *A Cosmos in Stone,* as cited in Rushton, Neil. "Shamanic Explorations of Supernatural Realms: Cave Art - The Earliest Folklore." Ancient Origins. Last modified November 17, 2016. https://www.ancient-origins.net/history/shamanic-explorations-supernatural-realms-cave-art-earliest-folklore-007027.

Losey, Robert J., Vladimir I. Bazaliiski, Sandra Garvie-Lok, Mietje Germonpré, Jennifer A. Leonard, Andrew L. Allen, M. Anne Katzenberg, Mikhail V. Sablin. "Canids As Persons: Early Neolithic Dog and Wolf Burials, Cis-Baikal, Siberia." ScienceDirect. https://core.ac.uk/download/pdf/36077923.pdf 2011.

Massachusetts Institute Of Technology. "Primitive Brain Is 'Smarter' Than We Think, MIT Study Shows." ScienceDaily. Acessed March 4, 2020. www.sciencedaily.com/releases/2005/03/050308134448.htm.

McCoy, Daniel. "Odin." Norse Mythology for Smart People. Accessed June 2019. https://norse-mythology.org/gods-and-creatures/the-aesir-gods-and-goddesses/odin/.

Naumann, Robert, Janie M. Ondracek, Samuel Reiter, Mark Shein-Idelson, Maria Antonietta Tosches, Tracy M Yamawaki and Giles Laurent. "The Reptilian Brain." US National Library of Medicine National Institutes of Health. Last modified April 20, 2015. https://www.ncbi.nlm.nih.gov/pmc/articles/PMC4406946/.

Rushton, Neil. "Shamanic Explorations of Supernatural Realms: Cave Art - The Earliest Folklore." Ancient Origins. Last modified November 17, 2016. https://www.ancient-origins.net/history/shamanic-explorations-supernatural-realms-cave-art-earliest-folklore-007027.

Sargent, Denny. "Nani Doro, The Way of the Siberian Ulchi Shaman." Feral Magick Blog. Last modified December 18, 2019. https://dennysargentauthor.com/nani-doro-the-way-of-the-siberian-ulchi-shaman/.

Wolf Worlds. "Types of Wolves." Wolf Worlds. Accessed 2019. https://www.wolfworlds.com/types-of-wolves/.

To Write to the Author

If you wish to contact the author or would like more information about this book, please write to the author in care of Llewellyn Worldwide Ltd. and we will forward your request. Both the author and publisher appreciate hearing from you and learning of your enjoyment of this book and how it has helped you. Llewellyn Worldwide Ltd. cannot guarantee that every letter written to the author can be answered, but all will be forwarded. Please write to:

Denny Sargent
℅ Llewellyn Worldwide
2143 Wooddale Drive
Woodbury, MN 55125-2989

Please enclose a self-addressed stamped envelope for reply,
or $1.00 to cover costs. If outside the U.S.A., enclose
an international postal reply coupon.

Many of Llewellyn's authors have websites with additional
information and resources. For more information,
please visit our website at http://www.llewellyn.com